ADVANCE

Saint Junipero Serra's Camino

"Stephen Binz has written a great practical guidebook for exploring the California missions and the spiritual legacy of St. Junípero Serra. I pray that this book will lead many people to rediscover the ancient practice of the pilgrimage and to renew their commitment to the new evangelization of California and the American continent."

—Most Reverend José H. Gomez, archbishop of Los Angeles

"Just as for centuries pilgrims have walked the Camino de Santiago de Compostela in Spain, this concise volume will encourage a similar Camino to the twenty-one missions in our state. Binz's California history is correct, his prayer-guide devotional, and his artistic descriptions captivating."

—Michael C. Barber, S.J., bishop of Oakland

"I am most pleased to endorse this superb and very timely new book written by Stephen J. Binz. I see this book as a tremendous addition to our library of significant works telling the story of the life and legacy of St. Junipero Serra and his companions, and helping us in trying to build bridges."

—Richard J. Garcia, bishop of Monterey

"I am very grateful to recommend this work of Stephen J. Binz.... I find that his personal descriptions of the missions beautifully describe the reality of Faith, prayer and history that is evident at each of the missions. This is especially true of Mission San Juan Capistrano, where I frequently visit as the bishop of the diocese where this mission is located, and where I like to stop and pray in the 'Serra Chapel'."

—Kevin W. Vann, bishop of Orange

"Part hagiography of a courageous missionary, part honest historical reference, and part handy travelogue, Stephen Binz's *Saint Junipero Serra's Camino* is first and foremost a spiritual preparation and call to action in our own sharing of the Good News of the Gospel. With keen detail and deep spirituality, Binz encourages each of us to fully embrace our role in the New Evangelization by following in the footsteps of California's spiritual giant, St. Junipero Serra. This Californian can't wait to journey with Binz to discover Father Serra's journey in bringing the faith to my home state and beyond!"

—LISA M. HENDEY, founder of the Catholic Mom blog and author of the Chime Travelers series

"What an extraordinary pilgrim's guide this is! This book shows how to maximize a pilgrimage experience and make its graces and challenges a part of one's ongoing spiritual development. It is invaluable for anyone wanting to understand Junípero Serra."

—MURRAY BODO, OFM, author, *Francis: The Journey and the Dream*

"Few writers are as dependably accessible and warmly instructive as Stephen Binz. Anyone looking for a new way of pursuing spiritual growth, and a generous introduction to one of the Church's newest saints, will be enriched by this wonderful book."

—ELIZABETH SCALIA, editor-in-chief at Aleteia and author, *Strange Gods: Unmasking the Idols in Everyday Life*

"Stephen Binz has written an excellent volume. It makes an important contribution to popular studies of Saint Junipero

Serra, and it will be a great help to people who are visiting the California missions."

—ROBERT SENKEWICZ, professor of history at Santa Clara University, author, *Junípero Serra: California, Indians, and the Transformation of a Missionary*

"Stephen J. Binz has studied and learned the purpose of the California missions and their place in the history of the West Coast of America. I welcome this book and pray that it will assist future readers to assimilate and further the notion of evangelization, and how it will figure into the final analysis of missionary work along El Camino Real."

—MSGR. FRANCIS J. WEBER, scholar of California Catholic history

"I recommend this book to everybody, whether you are journeying along the California Camino or staying in the comfort of your own home. This is an all-in-one and must-have resource for anyone interested in learning more about the missions and the newest American Saint who founded them."

—DANIEL P. HORAN, OFM, author, *The Franciscan Heart of Thomas Merton*

"This book by Stephen J. Binz provides a timely, comprehensive, and liturgically invaluable resource for those seeking to balance the historical and spiritual dimensions of their experience.... Binz effectively guides the reader through the evangelization of California by way of a heartfelt reconciliation of words, deeds, prayers, and cultural histories not often appreciated in today's increasingly secular world."

—RUBÉN G. MENDOZA, PhD, RPA, California State University, author, *The California Missions Source Book*

"In California our El Camino and its missions offers wayfarer pilgrims a range of meaningful experiences and relevant insight into the life of California's Founding Father, Saint Junípero Serra.... From rugged coastlines to serene vast valleys, each step of El Camino is at the crossroads of history serving as a living rosary chain of our faith. Definitely recommend for those taking the journey."

—JEWEL-SEAN YAHUT GENTRY, MA Ed., California Missions Coordinator, Diocese of Monterey, Carmel

"*Saint Junipero Serra's Camino* by Stephen Binz is an excellent guide for the pilgrim who wants to walk with the saint. I heartily endorse the book."

—JOHN CELLA, OFM, director of Franciscan Pilgrimage Programs

"An excellent resource for catechetical ministers and for all who align their lives more closely with the Gospel of Jesus and embark on the journey of transformation as missionary disciples."

—EDITH PRENDERGAST, RSC, former director of religious education, archdiocese of Los Angeles

SAINT JUNIPERO SERRA'S CAMINO

A PILGRIMAGE GUIDE TO THE CALIFORNIA MISSIONS

STEPHEN J. BINZ

franciscan
media

Scripture passages have been taken from *New Revised Standard Version Bible*, Catholic edition, copyright ©1989 by the Division of Christian Education of the National Council of the Churches of Christ in the U.S.A., and used by permission. All rights reserved.

Cover and book design by Mark Sullivan
Cover and interior photos © Stephen J. Binz. Used by permission.

ISBN 978-1-63253-128-5

Published by Franciscan Media
28 W. Liberty St.
Cincinnati, OH 45202
www.FranciscanMedia.org

To Serra International,
dedicated to the promotion of vocations
to the priesthood and religious life.

Contents

CHAPTER ONE

Franciscan missionaries bringing the Gospel to California

The Pilgrimage Camino through the Missions of California

Traveling along the coast of California and reading the names of places that grew out of the missions is like reciting a litany of the saints: San Diego, San Juan Capistrano, Santa Bárbara, San Luis Obispo, San José, Santa Clara, San Francisco. The heroic lives of these ancient saints inspired the Franciscan missionaries to carry the Christian Gospel to the New World with evangelizing passion.

The missions—twenty-one in number, beginning in San Diego and stretching to Sonoma, north of San Francisco Bay—were the inspiration of St. Junípero Serra. As he envisioned them, the missions would form a holy ladder, with rungs placed conveniently up and down the coast. This "royal way"—El Camino Real—holds the tangible memories of the days when Christianity first came to California.

The Camino of St. Junípero Serra links the missions as a pilgrimage route. Begun as trails created by the California natives for travel and trade, this roadway was adopted by the Spaniards as they explored and settled California. Today, while much of it lies under the asphalt of Highway 101, in other areas it can be traced along city streets, rural roads, and still occasionally as dirt trails on mission grounds. The route is marked by a series of miniature mission bells—originally the work of the Native Daughters of the Golden West and the California Federation of Women's Clubs in the early twentieth century. These cast-iron bells have been hung from eleven-foot bent guideposts, designed to resemble a shepherd's staff and to be easily visible to travelers.

St. Junipero Serra's Camino is an ideal way of pilgrimage. Like the ancient pilgrimage routes—the path of Jesus through Galilee to Jerusalem, the way of the early martyrs in Rome, and the Camino of Santiago de Compostela—it challenges the traveler to make a transforming journey, an *internal* journey that parallels the external trip. In traveling this road, pilgrims encounter holy places, communities of faith, occasions for meditative prayer, and prospects for inner healing—opportunities to align their lives more closely with the Gospel in order to become missionary disciples of Jesus.

THE MISSIONS AS PLACES OF PILGRIMAGE

Each of the twenty-one missions has been shaped and reshaped by grace-filled people for generations, and the memory of the early missionaries and their ardor for the Gospel pervades the grounds. The walls and ceilings of the mission structures express the Native American culture, with bright oranges, reds, yellows, and blues in geometric patterns. Iridescent abalone shells, spiritually powerful objects for the Indians, hold holy water in wall niches and adorn the tabernacle for the Blessed Sacrament. The sacrifices of the indigenous peoples built these places into thriving communities in which native talents were blended with European ways.

Yet those who travel along this ancient road experience not only slices of history, but opportunities to experience the presence of the living God in tangible ways today. All but two of the missions are functioning churches, where Christian baptisms, holy Mass, and beautiful weddings are regularly celebrated. The Sunday schedule of worship alternates between English and Spanish and sometimes includes services in Vietnamese, Haitian, Portuguese, and other languages for California's immigrant communities.

Each of the missions is a unique jewel and a spiritual oasis. Some are found wedged into cities; others are surrounded by mountains and valleys. The grounds are filled with bells, statues, fountains, and gardens, all symbols of life and feasts of color. Old Spanish mission art can be found next to Indian wall paintings, as symbols of piety from two centuries form a wonderful, holy mix.

Yet despite the missions' beauty and the Franciscan plan that each one would be a self-sustaining, utopian community, the missions were sometimes places of great pain. The histories can be difficult reading, documenting mistreatment and uprisings. Soldiers forcefully rounded up Indians in the countryside, killing men and abusing women, and some of the padres (priests) who administered the missions demanded heavy work and employed methods of discipline that seem excessive today.

As time went on, tens of thousands of Indians would die from European-born diseases. And despite the Franciscan insistence that they were holding the lands in trust for the Indians, the new Mexican government in the 1830s secularized the missions, essentially revoking land rights from the Indians and the Church alike. The missions decayed, and the Indian inhabitants were scattered, many being mistreated and killed with the coming of the Gold Rush and American settlers.

But, through it all, many holy priests helped to forge a heroic and faith-filled path through the region, bringing the truth of Jesus Christ to the native peoples. The Gospel message prevailed—and continues to do so today. St. Junípero Serra had a vision that did not turn out as he originally conceived, after human sinfulness overwhelmed the design, as it did in the Garden of Eden. Yet the Holy Spirit succeeded, and the missions today are sacred places, alive with God's Spirit and God's people. The faithful who inhabit and tend these missions can give hope to all pilgrims, that however flawed our own efforts are, the Gospel will still find a way.

AN INVITATION

I invite you to travel the Camino of St. Junípero Serra and experience the missions of California, as I have done many times. I will offer you suggestions throughout this book, but the quality of your journey will depend on what you desire to experience—and what you open your heart to receive.

Like the ancient paths of pilgrimage in Europe and the Middle East, this California Camino is a journey. It is marked with numerous stopping places along the way, each of which tangibly expresses aspects of the inner journey of the traveler. The more you seek, the more you will find. The more you ask, the more you will receive.

It can be as luxurious or as rugged as you choose. My first trip through the missions was in a rental car, driving along the California coast at my own pace, stopping to seek lodging at the end of each day. I've also led pilgrimages in luxury coaches, with nice hotels and dinners awaiting us each evening. And I've always admired hikers and cyclists trekking to one mission after another, as in the days before gasoline and electric power.

Far more than museums documenting the past, these are living places of encounter between peoples. In the same places where native and Spanish cultures came together in the past, people of different races, religions, nationalities, and backgrounds encounter one another today. Enter their lives along the journey.

I challenge you to go into the mission churches with a heart searching for God. Take the water of the font at each door into your hand, reminding you of baptism and the water of new life that God desires to spring up within you. Bless yourself, if you wish, as a tangible sign of the saving death and resurrection that unites believers in one faith. Light a candle at one of the altars, as a sign that your prayer lingers in this place after you depart. If you arrive and the church is filled with people celebrating a Mass, baptism, wedding, or funeral, don't turn away, disappointed that your touring has been impeded. But stand to the side, grateful that the faith these missions represent remains alive for so many today.

For people today are seeking the divine presence through tangible places, images, and rituals. Together they experience that reality in Jesus Christ, alive in sacred Scriptures and holy sacraments, reflected in stories of faith, the lives of heroic saints, the quiet of prayerful devotion, and personal encounters between people. If you have this book in hand, I suspect you are one of these seekers. Look for the ways that the Lord is risen and living today.

IDEAS FOR FOLLOWING THE CALIFORNIA CAMINO

Make an armchair pilgrimage. With this book in hand, you can easily make an at-home pilgrimage to the twenty-one missions. Take a day for each mission, supplementing your learning from the website of each mission and other links. Look at the online photos and explore the history and spirituality of each of these holy places. Enter into prayer, invoke the intercession of St. Junipero Serra and the patron saints of the missions, and ask God to give you the heart of a missionary disciple.

Pilgrimage by automobile. The easiest way to travel this route is by car with a GPS device. Begin in San Diego and make your way northward (or vice versa), exploring up to three missions a day at a quick pace or following a more leisurely schedule. Just enter the name of each mission or the address provided, and enjoy the journey through the beautiful scenery of coastal California. You can reserve hotels for the end of each day or, if you are more adventurous, you can simply seek nearby lodging along the way. Try to establish a balance between your informed reading of this guide and your leisurely and quiet enjoyment of the missions.

Pilgrimage on foot or by bike. Walking or biking the Camino of St. Junípero Serra is more difficult than the well-traveled Camino de Santiago in Spain, but walkers and bikers can frequently be found along the way. Though the trail is not marked for trekkers—and travel along busy highways is often necessary—some pilgrims have posted their own routes online for the benefit of others who may be interested in slowly traveling El Camino Real with a backpack. Traveling the eight hundred–mile path, from San Diego to Sonoma, including all twenty-one missions, you will pass alongside beautiful coastline, through cities and suburbs, along highways and quiet roads, through Central Valley farmlands, and across the Golden Gate Bridge. Helpful advice for planning and routes may be found at walkelcaminoreal.com.

Travel with a pilgrimage group. I've offered pilgrimages along the Camino of St. Junipero Serra through tour companies, bringing groups of twenty, thirty, and forty people along the way via luxury coach. On my website I post my upcoming tours, and numerous other travel groups offer this type of experience. By traveling with a group, you can benefit from a guide, offer prayer together in each church, and, if you travel with a priest, celebrate Mass at some of the missions. The group experience offers you the double advantage of a community of faith and experts to guide your way.

So, let the journey begin. Be inspired by the missions of St. Junípero Serra's Camino today, and prepare yourself to be enriched by two interwoven traditions: the Spanish Franciscan way—which affirms the goodness of creation and the incarnation of God in the world—and the American Indian spirituality—which practices respect for the earth and the divine spirit that fills it.

Discover in these pages the fruitful life of St. Junípero Serra, whose vision is responsible for this holy Camino. May you embrace his motto, *"Siempre Adelante!"* ("Always Forward") and let yourself become ever more committed to being a missionary disciple, always desiring to communicate the reason for the joy and hope that is within you.

CHAPTER TWO

Window of Mission Dolores Basilica

Siempre Adelante—The Life of St. Junípero Serra

When St. Junípero Serra was traveling northward to California, he encountered a group of natives along the way. Serra's journal account of that meeting reveals his deep commitment and emotions. He says that as twelve "gentiles" (the term used for unbaptized natives) approached, "I praised God, kissed the ground, and gave thanks to Our Lord for granting me the opportunity to be among the gentiles in their land, after longing for this for so many years." Then he blessed each one: "I placed my hands on the head of each gentile, one at a time, as a sign of affection," promising them protection and friendship. And in a reference to Jesus's invitation to his disciples to become fishers of men and women, Serra expressed the hope that "it would not be long before they allowed themselves to be gathered together in the apostolic and evangelical net."[1]

This is the essence of the life of St. Junípero Serra. This is what motivated his life and drove him forward. He was falling in love with the native peoples of California and bringing them the greatest gift imaginable: a relationship with Jesus Christ, a gathering into his Church, the gift of eternal life.

After that celebrated encounter, Serra continued his northward journey and entered California, where he would labor for God and the Indians until his death. As the Apostle to California and its Founding Father, no person in the state's annals has been more portrayed in statuary, paintings, stained glass, and other art forms. Monuments to Serra—including churches, schools, streets, a mountain peak, a freeway, and an earthquake fault—dot the map of California. Several societies have been established in his honor, including Serra International.

THE FRANCISCAN COMES TO CALIFORNIA

Miguel José Serra was born in the city of Petra on the island of Mallorca, off the eastern coast of Spain, in 1713. Educated by the Franciscans in his youth, he decided to pursue a career in the service of the Church and was brought to Palma, the capital city, to begin his studies of philosophy. In 1730, he was garbed with the Franciscan habit, which he would happily wear for the next fifty-four years, and the next year he chose his religious name, Junípero. The original Junípero was a thirteenth-century Franciscan brother, the "jester of God," a companion of St. Francis of Assisi, filled with joyful simplicity. Fray Junípero Serra continued to study philosophy and theology and was ordained a priest in 1737.

After receiving his doctorate in 1742, he was appointed to a chair in theology at the prestigious Pontifical, Imperial, Royal, and Literary University of Mallorca, best known as the Llullian University. Serra became an accomplished teacher and preacher, who inspired many in churches and classrooms through his eloquent persuasiveness and fiery earnestness. And there were promises of future advancement in the ranks of his own order of Franciscan friars.

But none of that interested Junípero Serra as much as a deep, enduring urge within him to share in the work of evangelizing the New World. So after much prayer and discernment, he requested permission to become an apostolic missionary, along with Fray Francisco Palóu. In a famous letter Serra wrote to his parish priest in Petra, asking that the priest inform Serra's parents about his becoming a missionary, he reveals the heart of his decision to leave his aging parents, his beloved Mallorca, his associates and community, and his university and academic honors in order to pursue the call of Jesus to "go forth and make disciples of all nations." Serra asked the priest to tell his parents of the "great joy" that filled his heart at becoming a missionary, knowing that with that knowledge they would urge him to "go forward and never turn back."[2]

Departing from the Spanish port of Cadiz, Serra and nineteen other Franciscans sailed for the New World, setting foot on the soil of North America for the first time at Veracruz in 1749. His next destination was Mexico City, a 240-mile journey. Although horses were available for the crossing, Serra and another friar decided to travel on foot. Without money or guide, carrying only their breviaries, they relied on Indian and Spanish hospitality for their food and lodging. During this celebrated first walk, Serra was bitten by insects, which caused his legs to swell and ulcerate, a wound that would plague him for the rest of his life. Limping painfully into Mexico City, he first came to the shrine of Our Lady of Guadalupe—where he remained overnight and offered prayers of gratitude—and the next day arrived at the Franciscans' San Fernando College to begin his missionary training.

After some months of intense training, Serra and a number of other friars were appointed to the Sierra Gorda region of Mexico, home to the Pame Indians. After learning their language, Serra won over many with his preaching, colorful liturgies, and gentle shepherding. In 1751, he was named presidente of the Sierra Gorda missions, a position he held for three years. At Jalpan, he worked for the economic betterment of the Indians, teaching them farming, crafts, and trade. He also worked with them to build a large stone church, which is still used for worship today by the descendants of those Pame Indians.

After being recalled to Mexico City in 1758, Serra spent the next several years serving San Fernando College and preaching in the churches throughout the country, traveling more than five thousand miles on foot. Then in 1767, King Charles III abruptly expelled the Jesuits from Spain and its colonies, much to the dismay of viceroys, governors, and missionaries. Soon the crown decided to entrust the orphaned Jesuit missions of Baja California to the Franciscans, and Serra was appointed Father-President of those missions. Disembarking at Loreto, the capital of the region, Serra offered Mass and began to plan assignments for the fifteen priests in his charge.

José de Galvez had been sent by the Spanish king as *visitador general* (inspector general), and when Galvez told Serra of his determination to occupy Alta California (the present state of California), Serra realized that this was the opportunity he had been longing for. He immediately volunteered to go in person— to erect the standard of the cross along the coast to Monterey— and he assured Galvez that many other missionaries would gladly join the endeavor. This was the reason Serra had come to the New World: to preach to the gentiles and to plant the faith on untilled soil.

Galvez and Serra began to plan the expedition that would bring the Spanish and Christian presence into Alta California—an initial exploration that would come to be known as the Sacred Expedition. In January of 1769, Serra blessed the ship *San Carlos*, as it began its voyage with a crew and twenty-five soldiers, bound for the ports of San Diego and Monterey. A month later, a similar departure was held for the *San Antonio*. In March, two overland teams set out, with Gaspar de Portolá as commander and Padre Serra as chaplain and diarist. Because of Serra's infected leg and foot, two men had to lift him onto his mule and saddle. No one could have imagined that this determined friar would labor another fifteen years along El Camino Real.

APOSTLE AND FATHER OF CALIFORNIA

Padre Serra began his diary of the expedition to San Diego and Monterey with a statement of purpose: "Diary of the expedition to the ports of San Diego and Monterey for the greater glory of God and the conversion of the infidels to our Holy Catholic faith."[3] For Serra, faith in Jesus Christ was God's greatest gift to humanity, a gift he had a desire and responsibility to share. And for the remaining fifteen years of his life, the tireless friar continued to live out his motto: "Always forward, never back."

Between 1769 and 1782, Serra worked in tandem with the Spanish military authorities to establish the first nine of the eventual twenty-one California missions: San Diego, San Carlos Borromeo, San Antonio, San Gabriel, San Luis Obispo, San Francisco, San Juan Capistrano, Santa Clara, and San Buenaventura. In principle, "cross and crown" were to work in harmony for the evangelization and "civilization" of the native peoples. As agents for the crown, as well as missionaries for the Church, the Franciscans followed the directives contained in the *Recopilación de Leyes de las Indias*, published in 1680. This compilation of Spanish royal decrees—a multi-volume guide found in the mission libraries and familiar to every early missionary—concerned the governance of Spain's territories in the Americas. Among its statutes were regulations meant to ensure the spiritual and material welfare of the Indians. Missionaries were instructed not to allow "the Indians to be forced, robbed, injured, or badly treated." If such occurs, "by any person, regardless of his position or condition," such excesses must be "punished with all rigor." Further, "the Indians are to be favored, protected, and defended from whatsoever harm, and these laws are made to be observed very exactly."[4]

In practice, however, the tremendous distances and poor communication between Spain, Mexico City, and the California missions bred misunderstandings and disputes. At times, it took nearly a year to ask a question and receive an answer. And, predictably, men in habit and men in uniform, those shouldering the cross and those bearing arms, clashed. Serra fought repeatedly with the military governors over the mistreatment and exploitation of the Indians. Writing to the Spanish viceroy in Mexico City, he was graphic in his outrage: "The soldiers, clever as they are at lassoing cows and mules, would catch an Indian with their lassos to become prey for their unbridled lust. At times some Indian men would try and defend their wives, only to be shot down with bullets."[5]

In October of 1772, after Serra as Father-President had founded five missions in California, he realized he was at the crossroads of the mission enterprise. He had made an overland journey from Monterey to San Diego, and there the deteriorating relationship between him and Governor Pedro Fages—an inexperienced administrator and a rigid disciplinarian—had arrived at a point of crisis. The lines of authority between Serra and the governor were not well drawn. Impatient with unnecessary delays, frequent bickering, disorderly soldiers, and above all, scandalous mistreatment of the Indians, the zealous Serra made the decision to return to Mexico to confer with the Spanish viceroy, Antonio Bucareli. It was a decision that would alter the course of California's history.

In February of 1773, Bucareli received Serra cordially and listened intently. The viceroy told Serra to put his petitions in writing to present to the court, so Serra returned to San Fernando College and began writing his report about the needs of the California missions. When the *representación* was complete, its thirty-two points covered practically every phase of activity related to the missionary enterprise, and Serra requested the replacement of the military governor and new regulations for soldiers, lest the development of the missions be impaired. Above all, he asked that the management, command, correction, and education of baptized Indians be conducted by the missionaries exclusively. Only "crimes of blood" would be relegated to the military for punishment—and punishment inflicted only after consultation with the missionaries.

After considering all the points spelled out by Padre Serra, Bucareli and his council approved them. Serra wrote, "Thanks be to God, in everything I was given a favorable hearing by His Excellency; he granted me all I asked for; and with that, I hope with the help of God that our holy Faith will be speedily and greatly extended, and the dominions of our Catholic King enlarged."[6] In writing this document and guiding its approval, Serra became the sponsor of the first body of law to govern early California. He was the first defender of the human rights of California's native peoples.

Before returning to California, Serra bade farewell to his brother friars at San Fernando College. Asking to perform an act of humility and respect toward them, he kissed the feet of each of them, begging pardon for his faults. His departure was his last, and he would spend the remaining years of his life in his beloved California. "California is my life," he wrote, "and there I hope to die."

NEW CHALLENGES

Two years after Serra returned from Mexico, tragedy struck in San Diego. Several hundred warriors from throughout the area crept into the mission compound, where they plundered the chapel, set fire to the other buildings, and brutally killed Padre Luis Jayme. Yet Serra, ever the faithful optimist, expressed gratitude that the ground had been seeded with the blood of California's first martyr. Thirteen of the attackers were imprisoned and sentenced to death, but immediately Serra wrote to the viceroy and reminded him of his prior request that "if ever the Indians, whether they be Gentile or Christian, kill me [or other friars], they should be forgiven."[7] The viceroy consented again, and the Indians, after receiving a punishment, were set free. Serra made sure that the padres had a visible role in the pardon, so the Indians could see that the Christians practiced the Gospel they taught.

In 1778, the Father-President received permission from Pope Clement XIV to administer the sacrament of confirmation to the neophytes of California, an authorization commonly given to those laboring in mission areas without the services of a bishop. Apparently there were discussions in those years about whether or not Serra would be made a bishop. Padre Francisco Palóu, Serra's first biographer, declares that when rumors reached Monterey that a "great honor" awaited the Father-President,

Serra resolved to refuse this distinction or any other that would avert his efforts to live as an apostolic missionary, "living among the gentiles and shedding his blood, if such were the will of God, in order to bring about their conversion."[8]

Yet, Serra was delighted with the authorization he received to administer confirmation throughout the missions. Adult neophytes were instructed on the nature of the sacrament, sponsors were sought, and plans were made for the sacrament at Carmel and Monterey. On June 29, the Feast of Sts. Peter and Paul, Serra administered the first confirmations in California. He began a new book of records, his *Libro de Confirmaciones*, in which he entered in his own hand the name, age, date, place, and sponsor of each confirmed individual. Serra then began his journeys to confirm the neophytes throughout the other missions, first setting out by sea to San Diego, both to celebrate confirmation and to encourage the missionaries in their efforts to rebuild the mission after its destruction. He administered 610 confirmations there, three of which were for the Indians who had killed Padre Jayme. He then went on to San Juan Capistrano, San Gabriel, and, after a long journey northward, to San Luis Obispo and San Antonio. By the time he arrived back at San Carlos in time for Christmas, he was exhausted, but rejoiced in having administered the sacrament to 1,897 people!

DEATH OF THE SAINT

In 1783, Father-President Serra traveled one last time through the nine missions he founded, continuing to confer the sacrament of confirmation on the Christian Indians wherever he went. He had poured out the better part of his life for the sake of the Native Americans—baptizing hundreds and confirming nearly six thousand people.

He had faced death many times, and it held no terror for him. In mid-August of 1784, Serra's dear friend, Padre Francisco

Palóu, arrived at Mission San Carlo to help him through his final days. At age seventy, the holy friar's body was worn out. His chest was heavy, and his leg was sore and swollen until the end.

On the day before his death, Padre Serra asked for holy viaticum and insisted on walking to the church. There he knelt on a prie-dieu, received the sacrament, then spent time in prayer. Later in his room, Serra called the carpenter from the presidio and asked him to prepare his coffin. He spent the rest of the day in silence, and that evening he was anointed, praying the litany of the saints and the penitential psalms. The saint spent much of his last night on earth on his knees.

The next morning at dawn, Serra was found seated in his chair, leaning again his bed. On his pillow lay the foot-long crucifix that he had carried with him since arriving in the New World. In the early afternoon of August 28, God's holy servant fell asleep in the Lord, shrouded in his Franciscan habit, hood, and cord. Palóu closed the eyes of his friend, then told the Indians to toll the church bells. They sounded the *doble*, the signal of death, to spread abroad the news.

The body of the saint was placed in the coffin, and alongside it were six lighted candles. When the door of his cell was opened, his beloved neophytes were already there with bouquets of multicolored flowers they had gathered from the fields to adorn his body. Indians and Spaniards alike entered in a steady stream to bid their holy padre *Requiescat in pace*. As evening came, his body was brought to the church, and the mourners kept an all-night prayer vigil. Many touched his hands and face with rosaries and medals, while others discreetly took small cuttings from the underside of his habit as a small keepsake of the man they considered a saint.

The funeral of Padre Serra took place the next morning, and Indians came by the hundreds from *rancherías* throughout the area. The solemn Requiem Mass was offered by Padre Palóu, with the Indian choir providing the music. At four o'clock in the afternoon, a procession was formed in which the body of the saint was carried around the large plaza of the mission, preceded by cross and candles, and when the procession gathered again in the church, the opening in the sanctuary floor was blessed and incensed. As the final prayers were offered, the body of Junípero Serra was lowered into the grave, where it remains today.

The Legacy of California's Saint

The exemplary life of Padre Junípero Serra was held in esteem by such a variety of people: friars, Indians, government officials, and soldiers, who referred to him for generations after his death as *el santo*—the saint.

Padre Palóu described him as a man who surrendered neither to infirmity nor to injustice. He concludes his biography of Padre Serra by describing the saint's life as a spiritual edifice, a temple grounded in humility and supported by the cardinal virtues. The heart of this temple, its holy of holies, is formed by his faith, hope, and charity. The love of God that burned in his heart led him always forward, never turning back. For he not only loved God, but wished that all the world might know and love him.

Serra's fame was formed of the virtues that marked his life: prudence, justice, fortitude, and temperance. Because of his genuine humility, he worked with the builders and masons, carrying stones, mixing mortar, and never hesitating to fulfill the humblest and lowliest of tasks. He was a man of strong affections, a priest of fiery yet tender zeal, capable of tears, but also of fury when faced with injustice.

In the end, he gave up all to attain his deepest desire: bringing the Gospel to a new world. A tireless, dedicated worker, he was a missionary of pioneering qualities, and no difficulty—physical illness, hardships in travel, primitive living conditions, opposition, or disappointment—prevented him from going always forward.

Padre Junípero was a heroic leader, able to rouse the spirits of his men and inspire them to valiant deeds. He judged their actions truthfully and fairly, gave correction when needed, and always led in asking forgiveness. His utter compassion and tender attention to the natives in his care was remarkable.

He loved the land of California and gave the best years of his life for its native peoples. He knew that he was God's servant, called to share in God's mission. And once he embarked upon that work, he never turned back.

CHAPTER THREE

First Mass under the oak tree at Mission San Carlos

Missionary Discipleship in the Way of
Sts. Francis and Junípero Serra

The first journey of Padre Junípero Serra when he arrived in the New World was to the Shrine of Our Lady of Guadalupe near Mexico City. There he offered the success of his missionary efforts to her intercession, for Mary, as Serra knew, is the Church's inspiring model for the work of missionary discipleship. When she appeared to the indigenous Juan Diego as Our Lady of Guadalupe, she was dressed like his people, spoke his language, and had the face of a *mestiza*, a woman of mixed race. The very purpose of Mary's apparitions to Mexico's Juan Diego was to draw the people of the New World to her Son. Both St. Juan Diego, Mexico's first indigenous saint, and St. Junípero Serra, North America's first Hispanic saint, are models for evangelization, dedicated to bringing about the reconciliation of cultures while leading all to Jesus Christ.

Following the Camino of St. Junípero Serra goes well beyond traveling his historical path through the missions of California.

It also involves imitating his missionary fervor, demonstrating always a loving understanding and respect for others and their cultures. Like our new saint who walked along the coast of California sharing the Gospel, we too are called to step forward in our daily lives and bring to others the Gospel of God's love. We are called not just to proclaim the Good News, but to *be* that good news; not only to invite others into the Church, but to *be* the Church in the world.

THE MISSIONARY EXAMPLE OF ST. FRANCIS OF ASSISI

St. Francis, the thirteenth-century spiritual father of Junípero Serra, was filled with a deep desire to proclaim the Gospel to others. God gave St. Francis extraordinary grace to preach with confidence, compassion, and clarity, motivated by a love for Jesus and zeal for the salvation of souls. Following the footsteps of Jesus, he demonstrated an unrelenting commitment to seek and save the lost.

Showing his own followers how to rebuild the Church, Francis of Assisi desired to be a living Gospel for all to see and hear, and, with single-minded devotion, even while burdened by frequent illness and bodily pain, he abandoned himself completely to the call Jesus had given him. These were dynamic traits that Junípero Serra shared.

While this following description of St. Francis comes from the first biographer of Francis of Assisi, the words echo into the life of Junípero, the eighteenth-century son of Francis:

> For during the space of eighteen years, which was now completed, his body had little or no rest while he traveled through various very large regions so that that willing spirit, that devoted spirit, that fervent spirit that dwelt within him might scatter everywhere the seeds of the word of God.... He filled all the earth with Christ's Gospel, so that often in one day he would make the circuit of four or five villages or even

towns preaching to everyone the Gospel of the Kingdom of
God: and, edifying his hearers not less by his example than
by his words, he had made a tongue of his whole body.[9]

By embracing evangelical poverty, St. Francis gave himself up
for the salvation of others. His love for the lost inspired him
to kiss the leper, to embrace the marginalized, to give all of
his riches to the poor, unbinding himself from the shackles of
wealth. This radical freedom enabled him to live in constant
prayer, submitting his body entirely to Christ and allowing God
to fill his heart with humility, compassion, and mercy.

Followers of Francis in later centuries took up his missionary
impulse and traveled continually further afield. One of the
greatest influences on this missionary movement was Ramon
Llull, a medieval Mallorcan who became a secular Franciscan.
Llull urged the study of Arabic and other languages for the
purpose of missionary work and traveled through Europe
establishing colleges to prepare future missionaries. He traveled to North Africa several times, and some traditions claim
that he was martyred there at the age of eighty-two. The young
Junípero Serra read the works of this medieval missionary,
which helped him to internalize Christ's call to go forth and
proclaim the Gospel to all nations. In fact, Serra was a professor
at the Llullian University in Mallorca, named in honor of this
esteemed Mallorcan. So great was Llull's influence on Serra that
he carried a small cross containing a relic of Llull, which was
buried with him at his death.

Another Franciscan missionary influence on Serra was St.
Francis Solano, the Apostle of South America, who was canon-
ized when Serra was in his teens. A Spanish Franciscan of the
sixteenth century, Solano traveled to the missions of Paraguay,
Argentina, and Peru, where he labored tirelessly for Indians and
Africans and against slave traders.

Following in the Franciscan tradition of these men and others, Serra would answer the call of Jesus Christ to bring the Gospel "to the ends of the earth" (Acts 1:8). As St. Francis knew well, God reveals himself and the plan of salvation through the missionary proclamation of the Gospel. And as his followers have understood, this salvation is implanted in those who call on the name of the Lord:

> But how are they to call on one in whom they have not believed? And how are they to believe in one of whom they have never heard? And how are they to hear without someone to proclaim him? And how are they to proclaim him unless they are sent? As it is written, "How beautiful are the feet of those who bring good news!" (Romans 10:14–15)

The beautiful feet of missionary disciples bring the Good News of Jesus Christ to the world so that others can hear, believe, call on his name, and experience his salvation.

Living Missionary Discipleship Today

The Church today teaches us that all of the baptized have two fundamental calls: the universal call to holiness and the universal call to mission. In the extraordinary lives of St. Francis and St. Junípero Serra, holiness and mission were one, unified in the joy of the Gospel. When we follow in their way, they show us the way forward as witnesses of Jesus in the world.

As disciples of Jesus, we experience the joy of faith, the joy of prayer, the joy of life's pilgrimage, the joy of detachment, the joy of relationship, the joy of service, and indeed the joy of salvation. Like Francis and Junípero, we find deep joy in following the command: Go forth and proclaim the Good News! Because of our call to holiness, we proclaim the Good News not only with words, but above all by a life transfigured by Jesus Christ.

When Pope Francis canonized St. Junípero Serra during his 2015 visit to the United States, the pope called us all to take on the joyful courage of our new saint, to leave behind our islands of comfort, and to proclaim Christ to the modern world.

> The joy of the Gospel is something to be experienced, something to be known and lived only through giving it away, through giving ourselves away. Jesus sends his disciples out to all nations. To every people. We too were part of all those people of two thousand years ago. Jesus did not provide a short list of who is, or is not, worthy of receiving his message and his presence. Instead, he always embraced life as he saw it. In faces of pain, hunger, sickness and sin. In faces of wounds, of thirst, of weariness, doubt and pity. Far from expecting a pretty life, smartly-dressed and neatly groomed, he embraced life as he found it. It made no difference whether it was dirty, unkempt, broken. Jesus said: Go out and tell the good news to everyone.[10]

Serra was part of a missionary team who went out to the peripheries—beyond the geographical, social, and racial boundaries of their time—to proclaim the Gospel. Pope Francis says that this call to evangelize must be a normal part of a mature, authentic, and integrated Christian life. The peripheries don't have to be far away. Evangelization is the urgent call of our Church: to renew, expand, and cultivate disciples.

Young people who are dissatisfied with the consumer-driven and self-centered culture of our time ought to listen to the voice of the Holy Spirit calling them to give over their lives for a noble cause, coming to know the great joy to be found in serving and in announcing the Gospel.

Pope Francis said that St. Junipero Serra embodies a Church which goes forth: "He was excited about blazing trails, going forth to meet many people, learning and valuing their particular customs and ways of life. He learned how to bring to birth and nurture God's life in the faces of everyone he met; he made them his brothers and sisters."[11]

Serra's canonization and following his Camino in California should prompt us to awaken our own missionary spirit. Taking with him only the certainty that God was calling him to missionary discipleship, he came to the New World to be a witness to God's love. As we follow in his way, let us keep his spirit before us, a vision of life encompassed in his motto recalled by Pope Francis:

> Fr. Serra had a motto which inspired his life and work, not just a saying, but above all a reality which shaped the way he lived: *siempre adelante!* Keep moving forward! For him, this was the way to continue experiencing the joy of the Gospel, to keep his heart from growing numb, from being anesthetized. He kept moving forward, because the Lord was waiting. He kept going, because his brothers and sisters were waiting. He kept going forward to the end of his life. Today, like him, may we be able to say: Forward! Let's keep moving forward![12]

—PRAYER— FOR MISSIONARY DISCIPLESHIP

Mighty and Merciful God, who has called your people to proclaim and teach the Gospel to all the nations so that your word may reach the ends of the earth, we give you praise for your missionary St. Junípero Serra, the apostle of California. As he served your Church and loved the native peoples of this land to the end of his life, may we follow his example, always going forward and never turning back. With all your missionary saints, may we walk the way of holiness and embrace the call to discipleship. We ask this through Jesus Christ, who is the Way, the Truth, and the Life forever. Amen.

CHAPTER FOUR

Faith encounter between Natives and Franciscans

Spirituality of the Native Peoples of California

The term "California Indians" is a convenient abstraction for an incredibly diverse population of indigenous peoples. Prior to European contact, the native people of California numbered more than 300,000, forming 500 distinct sub-tribes, each with its own territory and culture. Because of the temperate climate and easy access to food sources, they came from many different places over thousands of years, as the diversity of their languages indicates.

Even more diverse and abundant was the environment of California before the Europeans. Elk, antelope, and deer grazed the land, while wolves, mountain lions, bobcats, grizzly bears, and coyotes were common sights. Eagles and condors roamed the skies—along with flocks of ducks and geese—and herons, sandpipers, curlews, gulls, pelicans, and other seabirds filled the air near the waterways. Life in the ocean, bays, and marshes was bountiful: spouting whales, sea lions, otters, beavers, and clams, oysters, mussels, and abalones. Salmon and a variety of other fish swam the inland waterways, and fresh water could be reached by digging only a few feet.

The spirituality of the California peoples was marked by a profound respect for the land and water—and the animals that populated them. Depending on animals for food and skins, the natives of California spent a good part of life learning their ways. They worshiped animal spirits, imitated the movements of animals in their dances, and sought animal powers in their dreams. The Indians inhabited a world in which the animal kingdom had not yet fallen under the domination of the human race—a time before the rifle and European methods of hunting, farming, and raising herds radically changed the behavior of animals and their relationship with people.

RHYTHM AND RITUALS

Native Californians followed the ancient subsistence pattern of hunting and gathering, and most never tilled the soil or developed agriculture. They ate insects, reptiles, squirrels, rabbits, foxes, quail, dove, elk, deer, antelope, and more. They knew they lived in a generous land and trusted that the land would always support them. They made their tools from bone, shell, and wood. The bow, made of select wood and sinew, was every man's most valued possession, and arrows and spears were tipped with flint or obsidian.

Hunting for large game was undertaken with reverence and ritual. The sweathouse—where sweating, fasting from food, and abstaining from sex prepared them for the hunt—formed the focal place of the spiritual life for men. They went to sleep at night with minds open to dreams from the spirit world, hoping an animal spirit would appear as a hunting ally or to offer them advice. When the hunt began, the women and children stayed behind, singing sacred chants for the hunters' success.

Once animals were killed, the butchering and distribution of the meat was done with equal restraint and respect. After prayers and gestures of thanks to the animals, the hunters carried the carcasses back to the village, where every part of the animal was utilized: the skin for clothing and blankets, the antlers and bones for making tools, and the meat and inner organs distributed among relatives and neighbors. The hunter ate little if any of the animals he killed himself, as doing so would be considered crude and spiritually dangerous. Instead, he distributed it generously to relatives and neighbors. From beginning to end, the hunt was a spiritual exercise marked by self-discipline and reverence.

For women, the intersection of domestic and spiritual life was found in the making of baskets for both utilitarian and ceremonial purposes. The weaving together of diverse materials was an act of creation: willow, redbud, and grasses from above the ground, sedge and fern roots from below the ground, abalone shells from the sea, and feathers from the birds of the air. Patterns and colors formed bold and original designs, and important events like weddings and other rites of passage were celebrated with gifts of beautiful baskets decorated with beads, shells, and feathers.

For most of the California tribes, gathering acorns, nuts, seeds, roots, and berries sustained them throughout life, and the autumn harvest refilled the large basket-like granaries of the villages. Time was marked by the number of months (moons) and by the seasonal rhythms of the year, with one harvest following another in a yearly cycle. There were trips to the oak groves for acorns, to the marshes for geese and ducks, to the meadows for seeds, to the shore for shellfish, and to the rivers for salmon.

The various seasons and harvests were celebrated by religious festivals. Dancing and chanting were a natural form of remembrance, thanksgiving, and celebration. Dressed in their finest feathers, skins, and ornaments, dancers painted their bodies with red clay, chalk, and charcoal dust, and a chorus kept beat with split-stick rattles and chant, while spectators clapped with hands in unison.

Dances also marked the coming-of-age for girls and manhood for boys, preparation for battle and victory, and mourning for the dead. As with the hunt, participants prepared themselves for the dance with fasting, abstaining, and cultivating dreams, seeking to unite themselves with the powers of the spirit world and ward off the forces of disorder and chaos. Through the ancient dances and songs, balance was restored and the world was repaired.

SACRED VIRTUES

Strongly united to family, clan, and tribe, the indigenous Californians aspired to learn the traditional ways and pass them on to the next generation.

A person's identity, strength, and fulfillment were found in belonging. Any attempts at "individual freedom" were understood as a weakening of these bonds and made them spiritually vulnerable. From birth to death, life was a following in the path of the elders, the way that had been received from the sacred past.

The primary social value for the Indians was generosity. A wealthy family was expected to give generously to the many feasts and festivals of the community. The seed-gathering woman did not store the harvest for her own family, but distributed it generously. The hunter gained more wealth and security by giving away the meat for the good of the neighbors, rather than eating it all himself. Instead of perpetuating wealth in families through inheritance, the possessions of the deceased were often destroyed or buried with the corpse.

Moderation and restraint were essential qualities. Competitiveness was not a virtue, and boasting and greediness indicated that one was unbalanced and dangerous. It was a hard-working, restrained, humble, and generous person who would obtain praise and honor from his tribe.

Hospitality was also a prime virtue, and the early missionaries noted how a traveler would always be offered whatever food was available in the home. The sick, elderly, and poor were always taken care of by their families and the community. Stealing cast great shame on the thief's family, and the greedy and hostile person would be cast out, surviving as best he could on his own and serving as a cautionary lesson to the young.

Within such small societies, law enforcement was unnecessary. Good behavior was taught by the example and nearly unanimous conviction of the community. The chief of the village had the role of maintaining the traditions and ancient balance between the community and its gods. The people would give their chief privileges and wealth, but expected him to be a model of exemplary behavior for others. He cared generously for those unable to care for themselves: the blind and lame, widows and orphans and the elderly. Whenever guests or traders came to the village, he played the role of hospitable host, and he also served as master of ceremonies for the many festivals, dances, and ceremonies held throughout the cycle of the year. His rule was to be conducted by the virtues of the community: humility, moderation, and balance.

Old people were treated with the greatest respect of all. Within them, the memory of the community was stored. Their wisdom contained the spiritual stories, cycle of dances, plant and animal lore, family relationships, and location of sacred places. Caring for the elderly was the duty of all and part of the community's unchangeable way of life.

THE POWER OF THE SPIRIT WORLD

Rising at dawn, the indigenous peoples stood at the entrance of their dwellings and faced the east. They shouted words of greeting and joyful encouragement to the rising sun. The winter solstice was a time for special rituals, in which periodic offerings, like beads, shells, and smoke from tobacco, were made to the sun.

In the worldview of the California peoples, everything possessed a spiritual essence, with no separation between the spiritual and material world. Souls or spirits existed not only in humans, but in the sun, moon, stars, mountains, springs, and rivers, as well as in animals, trees, and plants, and even in wind, thunder, and shadows. Human life, then, was lived in respectful connection to all of these beings. Hunting a deer, making a basket, walking a trail, and giving birth were all done in relationship to the world of spiritual powers.

The early missionaries often assumed that the native peoples had no religion because their beliefs were so pervasive. Religion was not something that could be isolated from daily life, for, in a world in which everything had power, every act was religious. What mattered most was getting along with the animal-gods, acquiring their power, and using that power in daily relationships with others.

Surely the Spirit of God was working within the indigenous people of California before the Gospel was proclaimed to them. God was revealing himself through the beauty and splendor of creation: "Ever since the creation of the world, his eternal power and divine nature, invisible though they are, have been understood and seen through the things he has made" (Romans 1:20). For this reason, people everywhere are attracted to the Gospel, God's saving plan for the world, when they hear it proclaimed. God has created a template within the human spirit for the seeds of the Gospel to grow.

The Gospel proclaims that all things come into being through the Word of God, the Word that was made flesh in the world. Therefore, all of creation reflects the truth, goodness, and beauty of God. This sacramental view of the world seemed natural to the natives because it has its echoes in their indigenous beliefs. When the missionaries brought the Good News of Jesus Christ, they challenged the idolatrous practices of the natives, but they affirmed their beliefs in the power of the invisible world. The catechism, sacraments, and prayers they were taught affirmed and personalized their own religious understanding by teaching them the universal power of the one Creator, the personal presence of God's Word in the saving life of Jesus Christ, and the pervasive power of the Holy Spirit.

St. Junípero Serra expressed in his writing a desire to understand Indian spiritual beliefs. He reported a conversation with his young native interpreter, Juan Evangelista, as he was searching for ways in which those beliefs might provide openings for the Christian Gospel. For example, Serra discovered that the cross left by the explorers at Monterey was seen by the Indians to have spiritual power. Juan Evangelista recounted that the cross was bright and beautiful, changing its size and appearance as they viewed it, rising up to the heavens at night. The Indians hung offerings upon it and cast broken arrows at its base. Serra also realized similarities between their native talismans and medals to the saints, and between their traditional songs and Christian chants. The diaries show examples of how he and other missionaries used traditional beliefs as springboards for their preaching the Gospel.

The Gospels and Acts of the Apostles show how Jesus and the apostles tailored the message to address different groups of people, as the growth of Christianity from a Jewish sect to a worldwide Church required the Gospel to engage new cultural groups at each point along the way. As a Christian evangelizer of his time, Serra also understood how beginning with people's own experience was the best way to proclaim the Good News.

Missionaries today emphasize the importance of enculturation, the creative and dynamic relationship between the Christian faith and a people's culture. They must learn from the culture in which they are sowing the seeds of faith so that the Gospel is communicated in ways that make sense to people within their local context. For it is, indeed, both possible and desirable to respect indigenous cultures, while pursuing the clear goal of Christian evangelization: to infuse the culture with the Gospel and lead the people to conversion in Jesus Christ.

From our perspective today, we can see that the early missionaries of California were often too immersed in their own European culture to clearly see the richness of the culture they were entering. Unfortunately, evangelization was at times insufficiently distinguished from colonization, and, for this reason, many Native Americans blame the Church for the loss of their own culture and identity.

To be global Christians today, we have to learn to see that the Good News of Jesus Christ lives in a multitude of cultural contexts, realizing that human messengers are never free from the cultural influences of their upbringing or the sociocultural attitudes of their day. But the lessons of the past oblige us to be humble in examining the beliefs and customs of others in order to bring Jesus Christ to a culture different from our own.

Today, Christian Indians seek ways of being equal participants in the life and mission of the Church—as indigenous people. They continue to explore ways to experience the freedom and spiritual power of the Gospel, while still fully embracing their tribal identity, traditional customs, and cultural ways in their expressions of faith in Jesus Christ.

As we embrace a multicultural Church, as it exists today in California and in our own local context, let us rejoice in the Gospel of freedom and life. As we celebrate our universal Christian faith, expressed through the values, languages, customs, art, music, and rituals of Native America, Spain, Mexico, and a host of Asian, African, and European cultures, we continue to follow in a special way the Camino of St. Junípero Serra.

CHAPTER FIVE

Room where St. Junípero Serra died,
Mission San Carlos Borromeo de Carmelo

Acknowledging the Past and Working toward Healing

*W*hat made St. Junípero Serra leave his home and country, his family, university chair, and Franciscan community in Mallorca to go to the ends of the earth? It was certainly his heartfelt desire to share with those farthest away the gift of encountering Jesus Christ. At San Diego, on the morning of July 16, 1769, as the soldiers raised the cross and Serra blessed it, Christianity was officially implanted in California.

As the mission system grew in those early years, the Indians were attracted to the missions by the friars and by other Christian natives. Upon arrival at the mission, they lived as catechumens. They were taught the foundations of the Catholic faith, fed and clothed, trained in new skills, and entered the routine of mission life. If, after several months, they had learned the catechism and prayers and desired to become Christians, they were baptized. The padres took on the responsibility of spiritual fatherhood for these children of God.

As baptized Christians, the Indians were required to live permanently at the mission and to learn to live a full Christian life in the pattern of the Spanish culture. They were given permission to visit their pagan relatives in the villages for a few days at a time. Often they would bring back others from the village who were interested in the faith, but runaways were sought out and returned to the mission to prevent them from reverting to their former way of life.

Each morning the Indians assembled at the sound of the bell, attended Mass, recited the *doctrina* (a compendium of Christian beliefs and prayers), and concluded by singing the *Alabado*. After a breakfast of *atole* (porridge), the morning labors were assigned, and each went to his work under the supervision of a friar, who often worked alongside. At noon, the community ate *pozole* (a stew), and a short period of afternoon labor was concluded with another assembly to recite the *doctrina*.

Serra and the missionaries were visionaries who came to the New World to set up utopian Christian communities, of which the Indians were to be the beneficiaries. In the original plan, the Indians would be drawn into the missions for a limited time only, about ten years or so, during which, under the fatherly guidance of the Franciscans, they would learn to pray, eat with spoons, wear clothing, and be taught farming, spinning and weaving, blacksmithing, cattle raising, and masonry. Most importantly, they would live their Christian lives according to the Church's sacraments: marrying each other, bringing their children for baptism, and living in holiness and peace.

After serving in this kind of apprenticeship, the Indians would be given land to own. Fully competent in the ways of "civilized" living, they would set up their own small farms near the mission, assembling each Sunday at the mission church at the ringing of the bells. They would serve as examples for the surrounding gentiles, who would in turn move into the missions to serve their catechumenate and apprenticeship. In time, the plan was for the missions to be handed over to parish priests—ideally from vocations among the Indians—and the missionaries would move on to more distant lands.

The Franciscans knew that European culture would soon be moving into California. Neither Franciscans nor Indians had any control over the fact that Spain, Russia, or England would soon occupy the land and control its commerce, and the mission system seemed to be the best way to prepare the indigenous people for this reality. In addition to living a life in Christ, they would learn the ways of European "civilization," and thereby fit into the new system as best they could—with their human dignity fully respected.

But history is never as simple as the ideal. Although Serra wanted only to do good for the native people, we must acknowledge the unintended consequences of Spanish evangelization. The natives were sometimes defiant and opposed the missions, leading to violent conflicts. Tribal cultures were mixed, languages were forgotten, dances and ceremonies were disregarded, and confidence in the permanency of the old ways was lost. Soldiers and colonists brought European diseases like measles, smallpox, and syphilis, against which the Indians had no natural immunity, creating devastating epidemics. The mission period lasted until 1834, a period of sixty or more years. Despite its undoubted holiness and heroism, the enterprise begun by Serra resulted in a cultural tragedy as the colonial period continued.

ENDING THE MISSION SYSTEM

As the Spanish empire declined, the Spanish influence at the missions diminished. When Mexico won independence from

Spain in 1821, the new republic enacted a series of secularization laws in order to grant property to new settlers. Using Spanish secularization as a model, the mission buildings were to be divided and the lands given to the native Indians. The Franciscans opposed these laws, however, insisting that their neophytes were not ready for secularization. Although it was the missionaries' objective for the native peoples to be spiritually and materially self-sufficient, the padres told the governors that these new laws were impractical and premature, and they knew they would be devastating during this time of political and social transition.

Whatever our view of the successes or failures of the missions today, one thing is clear: California Indians built each mission, and it was these native people who lived, worked, and died in them. During times of plenty and times of great hardship, these Indians got married and had children, passed down traditions and cultural knowledge, and experienced moments of great joy and sorrow. If the land of the missions belonged to anyone, it belonged to them.

However, as predicted by the padres, the natives were not yet sufficiently trained in the significance of property "ownership," and some were tricked into giving away their rights to speculators. The governor appointed an administrator for each mission, who gave away much of the prime land as he chose. Land grants for mission property, orchards, vineyards, crops, and livestock were secured by influential families, and the mission lands were quickly moved into private hands, effectively banishing the Indians. Overall, the political system was stacked against the Indians, and the missionaries were powerless to prevent the land from being taken away from them.

At the beginning of the 1830s, the Indian population living

at the missions numbered eighteen thousand; by 1839, fewer than one thousand remained there. As the support systems of the missions crumbled, so did many of the buildings. Some were routinely looted, with the materials used for private construction. Most often tiles were removed from the roofs. Without tiles and routine maintenance, the adobe walls began to crumble and often just dissolved through earthquakes and floods. By the time the United States acquired California in 1848 as a spoil of the Mexican-American War and took over the mission properties, the mission system had been effectively dismantled.

As hundreds of thousands of new immigrants flooded into California during the Gold Rush, hostilities between the Indians and other settlers rapidly accelerated. At first, Anglo miners, ranchers, and farmers saw the native peoples as a cheap source of labor, and many of the Indians found work as servants, miners, and ranch hands. Many other Indians formed small bands and took to hunting the horses, cattle, and sheep that had already largely replaced the elk and antelope.

Soon, however, the natives came to be seen by many of these settlers as a threat to their progress, security, and prosperity. Many new immigrants began to proclaim, in speech and in print, that the Indians were primitive and repulsive—and, therefore, expendable. After their need for a cheap labor force diminished and their desire to gain unimpeded access to the vast resources of the new state of California increased, many settlers began to regard the Indians as obstacles to be eliminated. And as the newcomers mined, hunted, and logged the Indians' most remote hiding places, natives began raiding for sustenance. This led to cycles of violence, as Americans, supported by new laws minimizing the rights of the Indians, organized war parties and sometimes slaughtered entire native groups.

The state's native population plummeted from about 150,000 in 1848 to only 30,000 survivors—an 80-percent decline—just twelve years later. The settlers waged a war of extermination against Indians, a race war that received the financial and legal backing of the State of California and the US government. The outright murder of thousands of California Indians during this period is one of the ugliest episodes in American history.

RESTORATION OF THE MISSIONS

In 1852, Bishop Joseph Sadoc Alemany petitioned the United States government, through its Federal Land Commission, to recognize as Church property those sections of the mission holding always recognized as such by the laws of Spain and Mexico. Through acts of Congress and court actions in the 1850s and 1860s, these lands were largely returned to the Catholic Church. The new Diocese of Monterey was not always able to take on the burden of maintenance, however, so some missions continued their decline.

Restoration of ownership did not translate into physical restoration of the missions until many years later, when the early twentieth century witnessed a resurgence of interest in the missions as essential to California's history. Several agencies assisted Church officials with the work of restoration. Paramount was the Landmarks Club, which was founded by editor and writer Charles Lummis in 1895 to preserve the old missions. Receiving no public funds, it operated solely with the contributions from private funds from around the world. In northern California, the California Historic Landmarks League was formed with a similar purpose. In addition, the Native Sons and Daughters of the Golden West offered considerable support for preservation projects. In 1948, the Hearst Mission Restoration Fund was established with a grant of $500,000.

These funds were divided among the nineteen missions owned by the Church.

Missions that were completely destroyed by time and weather have been rebuilt on or near the sites where they originally stood, while others, including buildings that date back to the mission era, have been restored—an ongoing project. The small entrance fees help to maintain the missions, and the donation boxes serve as a request to help in the restoration of these holy and beautiful shrines.

ON THE ROAD TO HEALING AND RECONCILIATION

History shows us that Serra was neither the perfect man envisioned by the pious, nor the vicious conquistador others contend that he had been. Likewise, the Indians were neither the idealized noble savages nor the demonized warriors. Serra was caring and protective of the native people, working to keep them from being mistreated or morally tainted by the Spanish military and government officials. Six hundred Indians were said to have wept at Serra's funeral, piling his bier high with wildflowers.

The response of Serra and his followers to the call to share the Gospel is a complex reflection of who we are and have always been as a Church: a sinful yet holy people constantly striving to follow God's will as best we can in light of our weaknesses and our strengths, with both our blindness and our zeal to be missionary disciples of Jesus Christ. As we follow the Camino of St. Junípero Serra today, let us work for healing, lamenting what went wrong in the past and acknowledging the real pains that remain. But let us also recognize the heroism of great men and women, native and Hispanic, who sanctified the missions of California and bear witness to their history.

The biography of Junípero Serra, written by Rose Marie Beebe and Robert M. Senkewicz, opens with a scene depicting an extraordinary encounter. In 1776, Serra and a small group of Spanish were struggling in a rainstorm along the Santa Bárbara coast, sinking into the ground as they walked. To their dismay, a group of Chumash Indians, one of the largest and most powerful tribes in California, appeared on the horizon. The situation was the perfect setup for an ambush, so Serra and his contingent expected the worst. But a remarkable thing happened. The Chumash approached, took the sixty-three-year-old Serra by the arms, lifted him up, and carried him some distance to solid ground. The amazed Serra later wrote, "I was not able to repay them for their efforts and their act of compassion, nor do I think I will ever be able to repay them as I would hope to do."[13]

This is the kind of encounter that Serra hoped to achieve throughout his California missions: Indians and Spaniards each seeing the needs of the other and coming to help. Pondering the encounter, Serra wrote, "And for me, this served to deepen the compassion I have felt for them for quite some time."[14] What would the result have been had this been the model of all such encounters?

While traveling along St. Junípero Serra's Camino, let us, too, learn to encounter others with mercy and compassion. Let these restored missions be places of reconciliation where we can celebrate the living community of God's baptized peoples, the Church of California that is Serra's greatest legacy.

St. Junípero's reverence for the beauty of California resonates with the Canticle of the Creatures by St. Francis, which begins "Laudato si": *Praise be to you, my Lord, through all your creatures, especially through Brother Sun, who brings the day, and Sister Moon and all the stars.* Serra's detailed observations about the trees and plants he found in California end with the same praise for their creator: "I have in front of me a cutting from a rose-tree with three roses in bloom, others opening out, and more than six unpetaled: blessed be He who created them!"[15] St. Junipero Serra was a Franciscan who truly echoed the reverent and grateful spirit of St. Francis. And surely the profound respect and spiritual power the Native Americans saw throughout the earth and the wondrous praise of God offered by the followers of St. Francis can together bring about a renewed world today.

As we follow in the way of St. Junipero Serra and enjoy the beautiful California missions, the questions before us have become the challenges of our discipleship today. Can the divine sparks still alive from missionary California come to flame today to bring about reconciliation and abundant life for the people of this land? Can the missionary past be transformed into something new that speaks powerfully and challenges the era in which we live? The rich spirituality of pilgrimage in the Camino of St. Junípero can arouse within Christian travelers today a deep desire to hope, work, and pray for a new civilization of love.

CHAPTER SIX

Tomb of St. Junipero Serra at Mission Carlos Borromeo de Carmelo

Inspiring Quotations for Pilgrimage

Quotations from and about St. Junípero Serra can be a source of inspiration and reflection along this journey. Here are a few choice excerpts from the writings of Padre Serra followed by a few passages written about him over the centuries.

QUOTATIONS FROM ST. JUNÍPERO SERRA

"I, Fray Junípero Serra, vow and promise to Almighty God, to the ever blessed Virgin Mary, to Blessed Father Francis, to all the saints, and to you, Father, to observe for the whole span of my life the rule of the Friars Minor confirmed by His Holiness, Pope Honorius III, by living in obedience, without property, and in chastity."[16]

—Profession as a Franciscan, 1731

"Well, then, Christians! Who is not going to have a tremendous love for the trials and tribulations with which the Lord, as a benign father, afflicts us in this life? Who is not going to embrace them with great zeal and to consider himself most fortunate to experience them? Who is not going to confess that God, in parceling them out to us, is sweet and gentle and that he is impelled to send them to us by his love? When we have travails, we have God himself at our side. *The Lord is near to the brokenhearted.* If we are lukewarm and have difficulty bearing those travails, let us call upon the Lord. In his compassion, he will promptly listen. The royal prophet, based on his own experience, testifies to this: *In my distress I cried to the Lord and he answered me.* The Lord sends us tribulations, because he loves us. Because of that love, he makes our tribulations more gentle. *Taste and see.*"[17]

—Sermons to the Poor Clares of Palma, 1744

"My beloved friend, I am at a loss for words, yet overwhelmed by emotion as I depart. I beg you once again to comfort my parents. I know they will be greatly affected by my leaving. I wish I could instill in them the great joy that I am experiencing because I believe they would urge me to go forward and never turn back."[18]

—Letter to the parish priest of Serra's parents in Petra, Mallorca, as he departed, 1749

"For I trust that God will give me the strength to reach San Diego, as he has given me the strength to come so far. In case he does not, I will conform myself to his most holy will. Even though I should die on the way, I shall not turn back. They can bury me wherever they wish and I shall gladly be left among the pagans, if it be the will of God."

—Diary of the Expedition, 1769[19]

"Along the way we saw hares, rabbits, and herds of antelope. But we saw even greater numbers of poor, lost sheep, that is, so many gentiles of both sexes and of every age. They do not run away from us as did the gentiles whom we met at the beginning. Instead, they stay close to us along the road, as well as when we arrive at a stopping place. They act as if they had known us and interacted with us their entire lives. This is why I do not have the heart to leave them like that, so I invited them all to go with us to San Diego. May God help bring them there. Or may He send ministers who can guide them to heaven in their own fertile and blessed land, which they have already been given."[20]

—Diary of the Expedition, 1769

"To get hold of gaudily colored cloth or any kind of rags, [the Natives] will jump out of their skins—as the saying goes—or take any risk…. What I would like to imprint deep in their hearts is this: *"Induimini Dominum Jesum Christum"* ("Put you on the Lord Jesus Christ.") May this be granted them by our most generous Lord and Father who clothes the birds with feathers and the hillsides with grass."[21]

—Diary of the Expedition, 1769

"Those who are to come here as ministers should not imagine that they come for any other purpose than to put up with hardships for the love of God and the salvation of souls. In a desert like this it is impossible for the old missions to come to the help of the new ones. The distances are great and the intervening spaces are peopled by gentiles. In addition to this, the almost complete lack of communication by sea makes it necessary that they endure, especially at the beginning, many and dire hardships. But to a willing heart all is sweet."[22]

—Letter to Father Juan Andres, from San Diego, 1769

"Our arrival was greeted by the joyful sound of the bells suspended from the branches of the oak tree. Everything being in readiness, and having put on alb and stole, and kneeling down with all the men toward the altar, I intoned the hymn *Veni, Creator Spiritus*, at the conclusion of which, and after invoking the help of the Holy Spirit on everything we were about to perform, I blessed the salt and the water. Then we all made our way to a gigantic cross which was all in readiness and lying on the ground. With everyone lending a hand we set it in an upright position. I sang the prayers for its blessing. We set it in the ground and then, with all the tenderness of our hearts, we venerated it. I sprinkled with holy water all the fields around. And thus, after raising aloft the standard of the King of Heaven, we unfurled the flag of our Catholic Monarch likewise. As we raised each one of them, we shouted at the top of our voices: "Long live the Faith! Long live the King!" All the time the bells were ringing, and our rifles were being fired, and from the boat came the thunder of the big guns."[23]

—Letter to Juan Andres, from Monterey, 1770

"The spectacle of seeing about a hundred young children of about the same age praying and answering individually all the questions asked on Christian doctrine, hearing them sing, seeing them going about clothed in cotton and woolen garments, playing happily and who deal with the padres so intimately as if they had always known them…is, indeed, something moving, a thing for which God is to be thanked…. Every day Indians are coming in from distant homes in the Sierra…. They told the padres they would like them to come to their territory. They see our church which stands before their eyes so neatly; they see the *milpas* with corn which are pretty to behold; they see so many children as well as people like themselves going about clothed who sing and eat well and work. All of this, together with the way Our Lord God touches their souls—who can doubt that He will win their hearts?"[24]

—Letter to Antonio María de Bucareli y Ursúa, 1774

"If the Indians should kill a missionary, what good are we going to obtain by waging a military campaign against them?…

Allow the murderers to live so that they can be saved. This is the purpose of our coming here and the title which justifies our presence here. It should be conveyed to the murderer, after some moderate punishment, that he is forgiven and thus we shall fulfill our (Christian) law which commands us to forgive injuries and not to seek the [sinner's] death, but his eternal salvation."[25]

—Letter to Antonio María de Bucareli y Ursúa, 1775

"The potential for accomplishing what I have wanted was always great, and now it is even greater, which is to complete, between the Presidio of San Diego and the Presidio of Monterey, a ladder of missions about twenty-five leagues apart from each other. The principal objective is the propagation of the holy faith, but the project would also offer comfort for travelers and contribute to the more peaceful relations with the indigenous nations along the route."[26]

—Letter to Don Fernando de Rivera y Moncada, 1776

"Without any doubt whatever, Most Excellent Lord, in this my third and most recent journey along the Santa Barbara Channel, where we met with high winds, downpours of rain, and much mud, and where, because the seas were lashed by storms, and running high, we could not walk along the beach—which would have meant a great saving to us, both in the length and quality of our excursion—these poor gentiles required a new title to our consideration—they have waited so long for the blessings which have been delayed so much for them. Despite my lukewarmness, tears welled into my eyes when I saw with what good will they came to my assistance, linking me on both sides by the arm to get me over the muddy steep hills which I could not negotiate either on foot or on horseback. It was sad to think that I had not been able—nor do I know yet if I will be enabled—to repay them as I would for all their sympathy and trouble. What a pleasure it was for me to see them, in great numbers, walking along the road with me, and breaking out into song each time I started a tune for them to take up. When the first batch took its leave, a second group, watching out for the opportunity, would come up for me to make the sign of the Cross upon their foreheads. Some followed me many days. All of that, for me, added spurs to the feelings of pity which I have had for them these many years." [27]

—Letter to Antonio María de Bucareli y Ursúa, 1777

"In reference to the care we take of our converts—let me tell you, Sir, they are our children; for none except us has engendered them in Christ. The result is we look upon them as a father looks upon his family. We shower all our love and care upon them. And great was our joy when we secured a general amnesty for those who had set fire to the Mission at San Diego and had most cruelly murdered its principal minister, the Reverend Father Professor Fray Luis Jayme. They are all now living in the said mission; they are held in high esteem, and receive every attention from the religious there." [28]

—Letter to Teodoro de Croix, 1778

"I have no doubt that with regard to the punishment we are discussing, there probably have been some irregularities and excesses on the part of some Padres. We all run this risk.... The trust they have in us is based on the fact that when we came here, none of them were Christians. And we have given them birth in Christ. We have all come here and remain here for the sole purpose of their well-being and salvation. And I believe everyone realizes we love them." [29]

—Letter to Filipe de Neve, 1780

"The only good quality that I can feel pretty sure I have, by the kindness and grace of God, is my good intention. As to anything else, what means have I of knowing whether I am right or wrong? May God direct us in the way of truth."[30]

—Letter to Fray Juan Sancho, two months before Serra's death, 1984

QUOTATIONS ABOUT ST. JUNÍPERO SERRA

"Notwithstanding his many and laborious years, he has the qualities of a lion, which surrenders only to fever. Neither the habitual indispositions from which he suffers, especially in the chest and in difficulty in breathing; nor the wounds on his feet and legs have been able to detain him for a moment from his apostolic tasks.... In very truth, on account of these things, and because of the austerity of this life, his humility, charity, and other virtues, he is truly worthy to be counted among the imitators of the apostles."[31]

—Pablo Font, OFM, a confrere at San Fernando College, 1773

"I have just received the news from our missions in Monterey of the death of our beloved countryman, the Reverend Father Lector, Junípero Serra.... He died the death of the just and in such circumstances that besides bringing tender tears to the eyes of all of those present, they all were of the opinion that his happy soul went directly to heaven to enjoy the reward for thirty-four years of great and continuous labors, undergone for our beloved Jesus, who he ever kept in mind, suffering them in an inexplicable manner for our redemption. So great was his charity which he always manifested toward those poor Indians that not only the ordinary people, but likewise persons of higher condition were struck with admiration. All men said openly that that man was a saint, and that his actions were those of an apostle. This has been the opinion concerning him every since he arrived in this kingdom. This opinion has been constant and without interruption."[32]

—Juan Sancho, OFM, superior at San Fernando College, writing to the Franciscan provincial of Mallorca, 1784

"He would always sleep embracing a cross that he placed on his chest. This cross was about a foot long. He had carried it with him since he was in the novitiate at the *colegio*, and he was never without it. During his travels he always carried it, along with the blanket and pillow. Wherever he stopped and also at his missions, he would place the cross on the pillow as soon as he would get out of bed. And that is where the cross was on this occasion when he refused to take to his bed, during the night or during the morning of the day he would deliver his soul to the Creator."[33]

—Francisco Palóu, OFM, *Exemplary Death of Venerable Padre Junípero*, 1787

"The history of the next fifteen years [Serra's years in California] is a history of struggle, hardship, and heroic achievement. The indefatigable Serra was a mainspring and support of it all. There seemed no limit to his endurance, no bound to his desires; nothing daunted his courage or chilled his faith... He yet remains the foremost, grandest figure in the missions' history. If his successors in their administration had been equal to him in spirituality, enthusiasm, and intellect, the mission establishments would never have been so utterly overthrown and ruined."[34]

—Helen Hunt Jackson, "Father Junípero Serra and His Work," 1883

"In these days of material progress, and with our whole nation regarding the acquisition of riches as the clearest proof of success, it seems to me that it is well for our youth to look closely into the lives of those men who constructed the foundations on which our State is built. Serra was a very simple-hearted man, yet in three special realms he claims the reverent attention of the youth of the State of which he was the first and greatest of a large army of pioneers.... Serra dared to do the thing that appealed to the very highest in his nature. He dared to fling himself in absolute and perfect trust upon God. He had but one aim—to serve God in blessing the people to whom he asked to be sent. He dared to be free!"[35]

—George Wharton James, *Heroes of California: The Story of the Founders of the Golden State*, 1910

"In the fascinating history of California, Serra, the brown-robed Franciscan, stands out clear-cut and ennobled as its greatest character. He is, indeed, one of the greatest characters of all history, a true priest, an ideal soldier, an evangelist, and empire-builder, a dreamer with a poet's soul. Travel, if you will, the seven hundred miles of El Camino Real, the "King's Highway—from San Diego to Sonoma, with its chain of twenty-one mission buildings; think of the labor of all that, the surpassing genius of construction and the marvel of its endless and intricate detail.... From the first moment he saw California he loved it, and as his eyes swept backward over the Bay of San Diego shining blue against the sea, and in through the laughing valleys and tumbling hills of the off-shore, he claimed them all for the God whom he adored with the wild passion of his soul."[36]

—John S. McGroarty, California's poet laureate, Los Angeles columnist, Congressional Representative of California, 1915

"The pathetic ruin at Carmel is a shattered monument above a grave that will become a world's shrine of pilgrimage in honor of one of humanity's heroes. The patient that here laid down its burden will not be forgotten. The memory of the brave heart that was here consumed with love for mankind will live through the ages. And, in a sense, the work of these missions is not dead—their very ruins still preach the lesson of service and of sacrifice.... Every Californian, as he turns the pages of the early history of his State, feels at times that he can hear the echo of the Angelus bells of the missions, and amid the din of the money-madness of these latter days, can find a response in 'the better angels of his nature.'"[37]

—John F. Davis, *California Romantic and Resourceful*, 1914

"The real Serra was indeed a remarkable man. Already at an advanced age when he came to Alta California, he nevertheless possessed the traits which where most needed in the pioneer. He was an enthusiastic, battling, almost quarrelsome, fearless, keen-witted, fervidly devout, unselfish, single-minded missionary. He subordinated everything, and himself most of all, to the demands of his evangelical task as he understood it."[38]

—Charles E. Chapman, *A History of California:*
The Spanish Period, 1921

"This man whose memory is indissolubly one with the epic of California, was great in humility. He triumphed by his courage, when everything would have appeared bound to discourage him and beat him down. He is one who is worthy of first place among the immortal heroes who created our nation. So his memory will never die, and his name will be blessed from generation to generation."[39]

—Isidore Dockweiler, California lawyer and politician, 1931

"In a sense Serra attained a certain immortality in memory. His fame has grown since his death, particularly since 1849. Monuments to him line his Camino Real from Petra to San Francisco. His missions have been restored—about a million people from all parts of the globe visit them annually. His name is a household word in California. He is a candidate for sainthood. This man who was so vital in life has projected vitality even from the grave."[40]

—Maynard J. Geiger, OFM, *Life and Times of*
Fray Junípero Serra, OFM, 1959

"The Lord has said to us that unless the grain of wheat falls to the ground and dies, it remains alone, but if it dies it bears much

fruit. So, from this holy seed, which is the mortal remains of Fray Junípero Serra, buried here beneath us, has come the flourishing and flowering of the Church of California."[41]
—Cardinal Timothy Manning, archbishop of Los Angeles, gathered with the California bishops at Mission Carmel, 1984

"Father Serra is one of the heroes of our land. His tireless work for the Indians of California, despite distances and physical disabilities that would have daunted a lesser man, remains a shining page in our history. His missions stand as a monument to his powerful religious convictions. I am proud that my own State of California has erected, in our Nation's Capitol, a statue in his honor."[42]
—President Ronald Reagan, 1985

"Father Serra and his fellow missionaries shared the conviction found everywhere in the New Testament that the Gospel is a matter of life and salvation. They believed that in offering to people Jesus Christ, they were doing something of immense value, importance and dignity.... Like Father Serra and his Franciscan brethren, we too are called to be evangelizers, to share actively in the Church's mission of making disciples of all people. The way in which we fulfill that mission will be different from theirs. But their lives speak to us still because of their sure faith that the Gospel is true, and because of their passionate belief in the value of bringing that saving truth to others at great personal cost. Much to be envied are those who can give their lives for something greater than themselves in loving service to others. This, more than words or deeds alone, is what draws people to Christ."[43]
—Pope St. John Paul II, Mission of San Carlos in Carmel, 1987

"Like Paul and Barnabas, like the disciples in Antioch and in all of Judea, [Serra] was filled with joy and the Holy Spirit in spreading the word of the Lord. Such zeal excites us, it challenges us! These missionary disciples who have encountered Jesus, the Son of God, who have come to know him through his merciful Father, moved by the grace of the Holy Spirit, went out to all the geographical, social and existential peripheries, to bear witness to charity. They challenge us! Sometimes we stop and thoughtfully examine their strengths and, above all, their weaknesses and their shortcomings. But I wonder if today we are able to respond with the same generosity and courage to the call of God, who invites us to leave everything in order to worship him, to follow him, to rediscover him in the face of the poor, to proclaim him to those who have not known Christ and, therefore, have not experienced the embrace of his mercy. Friar Junípero's witness calls upon us to get involved, personally, in the mission to the whole continent, which finds its roots in *Evangelii Gaudium*."[44]

—Pope Francis, North American College, Rome, 2015

CHAPTER SEVEN

The mission bells

The Twenty-One Missions of California

As I walk the grounds of each of the twenty-one missions, I always hear in my imagination the sounding of the bells. I envision the Franciscans and the Indians called to work, summoned to prayer, and invited to meals by the bells. From the first bell at sunrise, calling all in the mission to greet the day and pray the Angelus, to the last bell at night, the Poor Souls Bell, inviting all to rest as the evening grew dark, the sound of the bells marked the rhythm of mission life.

Bells were of many sizes, each with its own unique tone, and the combination of tones and rhythms was varied to ring out the many types of communications. It was an honor to be chosen to ring the mission bells, for the ringer must be skillful and reliable. The bells rang cheerfully at a feast or the union of marriage and tolled mournfully for the deceased. The bells served warning when danger was near and sounded notice of an approaching ship, a new visitor, or a returning missionary.

The mission bells have become an iconic symbol for the history of California and its missions, having been ringing throughout the state from its beginning. These bells mark the path of El Camino Real, memorializing the mission period and celebrating its restoration today.

Let the bells of each of these twenty-one missions call you to pilgrimage as you travel along St. Junípero Serra's Camino.

A GUIDE FOR EACH MISSION

To help guide your visits to the twenty-one missions, this book first offers you the street address and website to help you locate essential information, such as the opening and closing times. It then provides you with a brief history of the place, the story of the mission's patron or namesake, a notice about the mission bells, and a tour of the mission church. A brief prayer service follows, which may be prayed either in the church or outside on the grounds. There is also general information about the museum, the grounds, and other nearby sites of interest.

This guide follows the geographical order of the missions, moving from south to north. At the back of this book, you will find a map of California, showing the location of the twenty-one missions, as well as a list of the missions in the order of their founding.

"Mother of the Missions"
Founded on July 16, 1769
10818 San Diego Mission Road
San Diego, CA 92108
www.missionsandiego.org

San Diego de Alcalá became the patron of the bay that now bears his name when the explorer Sebastián Vizcaíno was mapping the coastline in 1602. He arrived in the bay on the saint's feast day and named the bay in his honor. The name was subsequently applied to the mission by St. Junípero Serra at its founding on July 16, 1769.

Because Mission San Diego de Alcalá was the first of the Alta California missions, it is designated "Mother of the Missions." The founding expedition traveling north from Baja California consisted of four teams, two journeying by ship and two by land. The second group by land, led by Gaspar de Portolá and accompanied by Fr. Serra, reached the bay and discovered that the packet boats *San Carlos* and *San Antonio* had arrived. The sight was both exhilarating and tragic. "Thanks be to God," Fr. Serra wrote to his friend Fr. Palóu, "I arrived here at this port of San Diego. It is beautiful to behold, and does not belie its reputation. Here I met all who had set out before me whether by sea or by land; but not the dead."[45]

Serra discovered that the camp had become a virtual hospital and cemetery. Many had contracted scurvy on the long voyage and were ill and dying. Some had survived because the Kumeyaay Indians provided them with game and food in exchange for their fabrics, which fascinated the natives. The

San José, a third boat carrying supplies and furniture for the missions, was lost at sea. Yet, the unrelenting Serra chose a site for the mission atop Presidio Hill and formally dedicated the mission. The spartan ceremony was attended by several other Franciscans, a small number of able-bodied soldiers, and several Indians from Baja California who had traveled with the expedition. The soldiers raised the cross, and Serra blessed it. Bells were rung. Mass was offered. And Christianity was officially established in California.

Once the exclusive domain of the Kumeyaay Indians, the fledgling mission was off to a slow start. The natives were naturally not attracted to a sick community and feared eating their food. They came to the camp only to accept gifts or to make off with unguarded sheets and clothing. Since the Spaniards were only able to communicate with the natives with signs and gestures, interaction often brought skirmishes. In August, the camp was attacked with bows and arrows, resulting in several deaths and injuries. When the soldiers returned fire with their muskets, the Indians quickly learned the fatal difference between their simple weapons and those of the Spaniards. The Indians later brought their wounded to the Spanish physician, who cured them of their injuries.

By March, supplies were running low, and the mission was still in a dismal condition. The relief ship sent back seven months before had been delayed in its return, and Portolá made the decision that the mission would have to be abandoned if supplies did not arrive by March 19, the feast of St. Joseph. The worried Fr. Serra proposed that a novena of prayers be offered in anticipation of the feast. After nine anxious days, the astonished group saw the sails of a ship on the afternoon of St. Joseph Day. Although the ship disappeared again behind the horizon, it sailed into the bay four days later to save the mission. Serra's persistence and confidence in God's providence enabled the mission to remain.

Five years after its founding, the mission was moved from Presidio Hill to its present location five miles up the river, for the Indians did not get along with the sometimes abusive troops at the presidio, and there was a scarcity of water. The new site, closer to the villages of the Kumeyaay, was constructed with logs and thatched roofs. But the mission still lacked the soil to support crops in sufficient number to feed the new Indian converts. So the neophytes were permitted to live in their villages and only come to the mission for work and to attend services. This situation did not provide the discipline required to form the natives in a new way of life.

The decision proved fatal during the night on November 5, 1775, when several hundred Indians from some forty rancherías quietly entered the mission compound, plundered the chapel, and set fire to the buildings. Several Spaniards and Indians were killed in the battle. Instead of running for shelter, Fr. Luis Jayme resolutely walked toward the attackers, urging them, "Love God, my children." But he was seized and dragged to the river, where he was shot full of arrows and clubbed. The courageous priest thus became the first martyr of the California missions.

When word of the destruction of the San Diego mission and the death of Fray Luis Jayme reached Fr. Serra a month later, he nevertheless expressed gratitude to God. Alluding to the early Christian adage, "The blood of the martyrs is the seed of the Church," he said, "I would welcome such a fate, with God's grace and favor.... Thanks be to God; now that the terrain has been watered by blood, the conversion of the San Diego Indians will take place."[46] While this death was a terrible blow to Serra, his primary concern was the continued growth of the missions and ensuring that forgiveness would be offered to the Indians.

While the governor wanted the attacking Indians punished by death, Serra insisted that they be pardoned: "All the evildoers should be forgiven after giving them a moderate punishment for their offense, which would show them that we practice the laws we teach them about returning good for evil and of forgiving one's enemies."[47] The death sentence was eventually lifted for the thirteen Kumeyaay men held in prison, and Serra asked that the priests be given a visible role in the prisoners' release so that they may be more receptive to the priests in the future.

In the following years, the persistence of the Franciscans bore fruit in the growing Christian community at San Diego. Serra wrote to Fr. Fermín Lasuén in 1778, thanking him for gathering the remains of Fr. Jayme into the new church that was under construction and expressing pleasure at the increasing number of baptisms there. Serra also reported to the viceroy that he had administered the sacrament of confirmation to three Indians who had been among those charged with the rebellious attack on the mission. By 1784, Serra wrote to congratulate Fr. Lasuén, who performed the thousandth baptism at San Diego.

After nineteenth-century secularization, the buildings decayed, but twenty-two acres of the vast mission lands were restored to the Church by order of President Abraham Lincoln in 1862. The mission was restored in the twentieth century, and the present church was declared a minor basilica in 1976 because of its historical importance. The mission church remains an active Catholic parish today.

PATRON OF THE MISSION

San Diego de Alcalá (St. Didacus of Alcala) was born around 1400 in a small town near Seville in the Spanish province of

Andalusia. He became a Franciscan brother and first served as a missionary in the Canary Islands, helping to convert many to the faith through his words and example. For the Jubilee of 1450, he traveled to Rome, where he attended the canonization of St. Bernardine of Siena. When an epidemic broke out among the friars living in the convent of Aracoeli, Diego attended the sick with great charity and trust in God. Despite the lack of supplies, Diego always had ample provisions for his patients. And he miraculously restored many of them to health by merely making the Sign of the Cross over them.

When he returned to Spain, he was sent to the Friary of Santa María de Jesús in Alcalá. When he felt that the end of his life was near, Diego asked for an old and worn-out habit, so that he might die in it as a true son of the poor St. Francis. He died in 1463, pressing a crucifix to his heart and repeating the words of the Good Friday chant of the *Pange Lingua*: "Precious the wood, precious the nails, precious the weight they bear." After his body was laid to rest in the Franciscan church at Alcalá de Henares, astounding miracles continued to occur at his tomb. His remains today can be found in the cathedral in Alcalá de Henares.

San Diego always had a deep devotion to the cross and a particular concern for feeding the poor. Once he was reprimanded for taking bread from the friary to give away, and, when asked by his superior to open his habit to show the bread he had taken, the bread was transformed into roses. For this reason, images of San Diego often show him holding the cross and a basket of roses. He is the patron of all Franciscan brothers and, of course, the diocese and city of San Diego.

MISSION BELLS

A tall, white *campanario* stands to the left of the church, rising above the mission gardens. The bell tower contains five bells. The three smaller bells at the top are copies of originals. The largest on the bottom left—called Mater Dolorosa—weighs twelve hundred pounds and was cast in San Diego in 1894. The bell on the right is called Ave Maria Purísima. Dating from 1802, it has a full crown at the top and was received as a gift from the King of Spain. All five bells are rung once a year on the Festival of the Bells, the weekend nearest the mission's July 16 founding day.

MISSION CHURCH

The simple white façade of the church reflects the spirit of the Franciscan founders. To the right of the façade, a long walkway covers the entrance to the mission grounds. There are nine niches in the wall, each containing a statue of the patron of the first nine missions founded by St. Junípero Serra. At the end of the walkway is a standing white cross, commemorating the witness of California's first Christian martyr, Padre Jayme.

The inside of the church displays a richly decorative style. The bright colors and hand-painted patterns replicate those used during the mission period. The carved *reredos* behind the altar is topped with a Spanish-style image of God blessing the world. Beneath is a dove for the Spirit and, in the niche, an image of the Virgin Mary and her divine Son. In the niche below is an armless crucifix that was never repaired, a reminder that we are his arms. The statues of Joseph and Mary, to the left and right, are period pieces carved in wood and then covered in cloth vestments.

In the sanctuary floor is a marble cross, marking the burial place of five Franciscan priests who served the mission. The intersection of the cross marks the tomb of the martyr, Padre Jayme, and the candle above burns continuously in his honor. All of these Franciscans died while serving the mission community. On the left side of the sanctuary is a polychrome statue of the Archangel Gabriel dating from the original mission. On the right side is a small statue of St. Junipero Serra holding a cross, which is from Mallorca, his birthplace.

The colorful pulpit has a canopy over it, indicating that the church is a minor basilica. The painting behind the pulpit is of San Diego, holding the cross and a basket of roses, and dates from before 1775. Of the bricks in the floor, the darker ones are from the 1813 church.

At the back of the church are the hand-carved front doors, and above the doors is the choir loft, entered by stairs outside the church. The baptistery holds a font that is a replica of that used in Mallorca to baptize St. Junipero Serra. The carved statue of St. Anne, the mother of Mary and patroness of all mothers, is the oldest statue at the mission, dating from the sixteenth century.

—PRAYER—

We adore You, Lord Jesus Christ, here, and in all your churches throughout the whole world, and we bless You, because by your holy Cross, You have redeemed the world (St. Francis of Assisi).

A READING FROM THE LETTER OF ST. PAUL TO THE CORINTHIANS: Brothers and sisters, the message about the cross is foolishness to those who are perishing, but to us who are being saved it is the power of God. For it is written, "I will destroy the wisdom of the wise, and the discernment of the discerning I will thwart." ...For Jews demand signs and Greeks desire wisdom, but we proclaim Christ crucified, a stumbling block to Jews and foolishness to Gentiles, but to those who are the called, both Jews and Greeks, Christ the power of God and the wisdom of God. For God's foolishness is wiser than human wisdom, and God's weakness is stronger than human strength (1 Corinthians 1:18–19, 22–25).

V: Holy Cross, whereon the Lamb of God was offered,

R: "Precious the wood, precious the nails, precious the weight they bear."

V: Holy Cross, wisdom of the foolish and strength of the weak,

R: "Precious the wood, precious the nails, precious the weight they bear."

V: Holy Cross, way of sinners and those who have gone astray,

R: "Precious the wood, precious the nails, precious the weight they bear."

V: Holy Cross, consolation of the sick and dying,

R: "Precious the wood, precious the nails, precious the weight they bear."

V: Holy Cross, pledge of new and everlasting life,

R: "Precious the wood, precious the nails, precious the weight they bear."

Let us pray:

O God, who redeemed the world through your only Son, by the precious wood of the cross, give us the grace to follow your will and to trust in your merciful love. Through the intercession of San Diego de Alcalá, give us a love for the poor, compassion for the afflicted, and the grace of a holy death. Amen.

MUSEUM AND GROUNDS

Exit the church on the left side and enter the gardens. The contemplative space features statues of St. Francis of Assisi, St. Joseph, and St. Junípero Serra.

The Father Luis Jayme Museum displays pictures and arti-facts from the mission days. The original copper baptismal font from the mission era can be seen, as well as vestments, statues, and vessels for services. An old plow shows how the fields were tilled, and earthenware demonstrates the water system for the mission. Notice the replica of the proclamation giving the mission back to the Church, signed by Abraham Lincoln.

Around the corner from the museum is the St. Bernardine Chapel (La Capilla). In niches over the door are four Franciscans: St. Francis, St. Bernardine of Siena, St. Junipero Serra, and Padre Jayme. The interior of the chapel contains an altar and choir stalls—brought from the Spanish convent of Santa Clara de Astudillo—that predate Christopher Columbus. The stone floor came from Our Lady of Guadalupe Basilica in Mexico City.

In the center of the outdoor quadrangle is the mission foun-tain made of Mexican granite, a reminder of the aqueduct system that brought water into the mission. On the side near the church is a statue of San Diego, holding bread for the poor. On the opposite side is a Kumeyaay hut, a horno for baking bread, and an archeological site.

Finally, next to the visitor center and gift shop, is the Casa de los Padres, part of the original friary where St. Junipero Serra stayed when he would return to the mission. The fireplace was added in the nineteenth century, but the furnishings represent the style used in the 1700s.

OTHER NEARBY SIGHTS

San Diego Presidio Site. On this hill is the original site of the San Diego Mission and Presidio, the first European outpost in California. When the mission moved upriver, the soldiers' fort remained here. The white building on the top of Presidio Hill is the Junípero Serra Museum. It is operated by the San Diego Historical Society and features displays about the city's history from the Kumeyaay, Spanish, Mexican, and American periods.

Old Town San Diego. At the base of Presidio Hill, the State of California has established Old Town State Historic Park to preserve the rich heritage that characterized San Diego during the 1800s. The park includes a main plaza, exhibits, museums, and living history demonstrations from the Mexican and American periods.

"King of the Missions"
Founded on June 13, 1798
4050 Mission Avenue
Oceanside, CA 92057
www.sanluisrey.org

Mission San Luis Rey was founded fourteen years after the death of St. Junipero Serra by Fr. Fermín Lasuén, Serra's successor as Father-President of the California missions. It was the ninth and final mission established by Lasuén, and it was the eighteenth of the missions established in California. As the largest and most populous of all the missions, it is deserving of its designation, "King of the Missions."

The native people of the area were known as the Payomkawichum, meaning "people of the west." Living in harmony with their natural environment, they harvested many kinds of seeds, nuts, berries, fruits, and vegetables for a nutritious diet. The men hunted for game and skins among the many different species of animals that inhabited the area.

The first Spaniards to see the mission site were members of the 1769 expedition, led by Gaspar de Portola. Fr. Juan Crespi, noting in his diary that it would be a good spot for the future establishment of a mission, described their initial encounter with the native people:

> There were more than forty Indians, naked and painted from head to foot in several colors, which is their usual custom when they go visiting or to war. They all came armed with bows and arrows, and their chief made the accustomed harangue. When it was concluded they threw their arms on the ground and sat down near us. The governor took out

some beads, and, giving half of them to me, requested that we two should distribute them among the Indians. They gave the governor a present of a few fish nets made of thread that they made out of some fiber which, when it is spun, looks like raw hemp. Behind the men followed the women and children, who numbered more than fifty, but they did not dare to come near. We made signs to them not to be afraid, and after one of the heathens spoke to them they came at once, and we gave them also presents of beads.[48]

Because of the friendliness of the natives, the area became a standard camping stop on the road connecting the missions, until the mission was established twenty-nine years later. So, when Fr. Lasuén founded San Luis Rey, the ceremony was witnessed by "a great multitude of gentiles of both sexes and all ages." Lasuén reported the details of the dedication to the governor in this way: "I blessed the water, the place, and the great cross which we raised and venerated. We then chanted the Litany of All Saints. Afterwards I sang the High Mass, during which I preached the sermon and exhorted all to co-operate in the great work. We concluded the function by singing the 'Te Deum Laudamus.'"[49]

Lasuén further reported that he baptized twenty-five male and twenty-nine female children whom the natives spontaneously brought to him. Seven young men and twelve young girls also expressed a desire to be baptized, but he told them that it was necessary first to receive teachings in the faith. Their instruction began that very afternoon.

The success of this mission for thirty-six years was due to the virtues of a single man, Fr. Antonio Peyri. He guided the growth and bounty of the mission from the day of its founding until its secularization when the padres were forced to flee. Peyri, as the senior padre at the mission, brought to his position an amiable disposition, keen perception, a prudent frugality, and boundless energy, as well as an exceptional talent for architecture and construction.

The ready desire of the Indians to convert necessitated the rapid construction of the mission buildings. In only six months since the founding of the mission, Frs. Peyri and José Faura had baptized 210 Indians of all ages, blessed thirty-four marriages, and buried five deceased. Thousands of adobe bricks were made, foundations were laid, and dozens of long beams were prepared for building. The work was expedited by order from the governor, commanding personal labor on the part of some of the soldiers from the San Diego presidio.

By 1825, the population at San Luis Rey was 2,869—more than three times the average of the other missions. In 1832, the total number of animals peaked at 57,380, including 27,500 cattle and 26,100 sheep, dwarfing all other mission herds in size. Under the guidance of Fr. Peyri, the main mission buildings were developed in all directions until they covered six acres. The culmination of his efforts was the noble church on a hill, which now dominates the beautiful valley.

As the secularization of the mission approached, Fr. Peyri requested permission to retire and return to Spain before the mission was destroyed. When his request was granted, he secretly left the mission in the dark of night to avoid the pain of farewells. But when the Indians learned that he had left, many of them rode at full speed to the harbor in San Diego to beg him to return, arriving only in time to receive his blessing from the deck. Many swam toward the ship pleading with him, as he sailed away.

With secularization of the mission in 1834, religious services were no longer held, and the Indians were forced to disperse.

The mission was sold in 1846 by the corrupt Mexican governor Pio Pico, and American soldiers used the buildings for ten years as an operational base beginning in 1847. In 1865, the United States government voided Governor Pico's sale and returned the land to the Catholic bishop. After a long period of neglect and destruction, an Irish Franciscan, Joseph Jeremias O'Keefe, was charged with restoration of the mission. Upon arrival in 1892, Fr. O'Keefe wrote:

> The houses were unroofed for the tiles and rafters; the beautiful arches were blown down with powder to get down the brick; doors and windows were appropriated; and finally, the bare walls were left standing exposed to all changes of the weather and erosions of storm and rains...there were no roofs on any part of San Luis Rey except the church and even that was gone in large part.[50]

O'Keefe's first task was to prepare living quarters for a group of exiled Mexican Franciscans who were given permission to establish a novitiate and college there. Religious services restarted in 1893 when the Mexican refugee priests, brothers, and students arrived. The quadrangle and church were completed in 1905, but the Franciscan novitiate was allowed to return to Mexico. O'Keefe continued the renovation until age and sickness forced him to retire in 1912. He is justifiably called the Rebuilder of Mission San Luis Rey.

Today, Mission San Luis Rey de Francia is an active Franciscan friary, a working parish, a retreat and conference center, and home to the Franciscan School of Theology.

PATRON OF THE MISSION
San Luis Rey de Francia (St. Louis King of France) was chosen by the Spanish viceroy as patron of the mission in order to recognize the relationship of France and Spain. King Louis IX

was the son of Louis VIII and Blanche of Castille, sister of St. Ferdinand, King of Spain. San Luis Rey is also important for the Franciscan tradition since he was a member of the Third Order of St. Francis and eventually came to be considered their patron.

San Luis was born in 1215; his father died when the boy was eleven years old, and his mother ruled as regent until he came of age. The young king always showed great compassion for poor and suffering people, feeding more than a hundred poor people each day from his own house, and fed many more on holidays. Often the king served these guests himself. He washed the feet of beggars, ministered to lepers, and always gave happily to those in need. When people scolded him for giving so much money away, he replied that he would rather his extravagance be in almsgiving for the love of God than in the pomp and vainglory of this world.

King Louis was known throughout Europe for his wisdom and fairness in administering justice. In the summer, he would often go from church to a nearby park and sit beneath an oak tree, where anyone could come freely with a case to settle. When faced with a problem between a rich person and a poor one, Louis always listened more carefully to the poor person because, he said, the rich have plenty of people ready to listen to them.

The king was a reformer who developed the system of French royal justice; he banned trials by combat in favor of trials by jury and introduced the presumption of innocence in criminal procedures. Louis wrote out his ideas of government in a set of precepts that he gave to his son, Philip. They say, in essence: "Love God, do justice, and serve the poor." As a great patron of the Franciscan friars and their evangelizing efforts, the holy king reminds us that Franciscan spirituality always involves a commitment to establishing God's justice in society and the promotion of peace.

St. Louis brought the Crown of Thorns from Constantinople to Paris and ordered the Sainte-Chapelle in Paris to be built to house the relic. He led two crusades: one to Egypt in 1248, which led to his imprisonment, and the other to Tunis in 1270, where he died from pestilence. Canonized in 1297, San Luis is usually depicted with a royal cloak worn over armor. His images often show him holding the crown of thorns in his hands.

MISSION BELLS

The blue-capped bell tower, which is seventy-five feet high, is the cornerstone of the entire mission quadrangle. The tower was used as a lookout, with Indian boys stationed there to signal messages with flags. There were originally eight bells in the tower, but now it contains two large bells, installed in 1939 and 1940, and a small bell installed in 1959. The bells are rung today only on special occasions.

MISSION CHURCH

The church's brilliant white exterior is an architecturally distinctive combination of Spanish Baroque and Spanish Colonial style, with Moorish influences. An image of San Luis Rey is atop the façade beneath the cross. To the right of the church, the entrance to the cemetery is marked by a skull and crossbones.

The church's interior is cruciform, the only surviving mission church laid out in this form. The long nave is crossed by a transept, which allows for two side altars, and the main altar contains a large wooden reredos. At the top is an original statue depicting St. Louis the King of France holding the crown of thorns. To the left and right are two archangels, St. Michael and St. Raphael. The central crucifix is from Nicaragua and dates to the eighteenth century. To the lower left and right are statues of St. Joseph and the Virgin Mary.

At the crossing, a dome is topped by an octagonal lantern with 144 panes of glass. It is the only such feature in all the mission churches. The side altar in the left transept is called the Ecce Homo altar. The main figure depicts the suffering Christ, scourged and wearing the crown of thorns. This unusual wooden sculpture, containing porcelain teeth and moveable joints, was created in nineteenth-century Mexico. The statue to the left is St. Francis Xavier, the Jesuit missionary, and to the right is St. Anthony of Padua. The altar in the right transept features St. Francis of Assisi. He is flanked by images of the Sorrowful Mother to the left and St. Elizabeth of Hungary to the right.

The colorful décor throughout the church reflects the blending of Spanish and Native American symbols and designs. The fourteen Stations of the Cross are from the eighteenth century. The baptistery—located at the rear of the church opposite the stairway to the choir loft—contains the original baptismal font used by Fr. Peyri to baptize new Christians. It is made of hand-hammered copper with iron hardware. The sculpture there is an eighteenth-century polychrome image of St. John the Baptist.

Off the center of the nave is the Madonna Chapel, which is octagonal in shape and covered by a dome. The central altar is recessed and holds an image of Mary Queen of Heaven, sculpted of wood, with polychrome paint and a brass crown. The chapel originally served as a mortuary chapel, and the doorway leads directly into the cemetery, which contains grave markers of early settlers, crypts of the friars, and a monument to the deceased Luiseño Indians.

—Prayer—

We adore You, Lord Jesus Christ, here, and in all your churches
throughout the whole world, and we bless You, because by your
holy Cross, You have redeemed the world (St. Francis of Assisi).

A READING FROM THE PROPHET ISAIAH:
Is not this the fast that I choose:
    to loose the bonds of injustice,
    to undo the thongs of the yoke,
to let the oppressed go free,
    and to break every yoke?
 Is it not to share your bread with the hungry,
    and bring the homeless poor into your house;
when you see the naked, to cover them,
    and not to hide yourself from your own kin?
Then your light shall break forth like the dawn,
    and your healing shall spring up quickly;
your vindicator shall go before you,
    the glory of the LORD shall be your rearguard.
Then you shall call, and the LORD will answer;
    you shall cry for help, and he will say, Here I am.

If you remove the yoke from among you,
    the pointing of the finger, the speaking of evil,
if you offer your food to the hungry
    and satisfy the needs of the afflicted,
then your light shall rise in the darkness
    and your gloom be like the noonday.
The LORD will guide you continually,
    and satisfy your needs in parched places,
    and make your bones strong;
and you shall be like a watered garden,
    like a spring of water,
    whose waters never fail (Isaiah 58:6–11).

V: St. Louis, holy and merciful king, who served the kingdom of God.

R: Pray for us.

V: St. Louis, confessor of the faith and ruler of a just kingdom.

R: Pray for us.

V: St. Louis, obedient son of the church and follower of the Franciscan way.

R: Pray for us.

V: St. Louis, protector of the weak and servant of the poor.

R: Pray for us.

Let us pray:

King of kings and Lord of lords, with thorns for a crown and a cross for your throne, you have welcomed us into the courts of your kingdom. Through the intercession of St. Louis, king of France, give us a passion to pursue justice, care for the weak, and build up your church with zeal. Amen.

MUSEUM AND GROUNDS

The museum contains artifacts from the Native American culture and objects—such as bells, cattle brands, religious statues, and sacred vessels—from the mission era. There are historical drawings, photographs, and paintings of the mission, as well as displays of weaving, laundry, the kitchen, and a sparse bedroom of the padres. The archways of the courtyard contain models showing the design of the entire mission complex.

To the left of the entrance to the museum, a view into the gardens of the retreat center reveals ruins of the original large quadrangle space. In the garden is a portion of the original wall with one standing arch, and through the arch you can see the first pepper tree in the state of California. It was planted here in 1830 from seeds brought by a sailor from Peru and continues to grow today.

Walk away from the front of the mission and down the hill to see the adobe ruins of the military barracks that once housed the Spanish soldiers assigned to protect the mission. With apartments and a lookout tower, the barracks housed five to eleven soldiers commanded by a corporal.

Walk further down the hill to view the *lavanderia*—an open-air laundry where the Indians washed their clothes and bathed—and descend the grand staircase to the washing area. Water from the San Luis Rey River was diverted to the site via aqueducts. Water flowed down from both sides of the stairway and spouted from the mouths of carved gargoyles into a series of tile and stone pools. The water was then further channeled to irrigate the mission gardens and fields.

OTHER NEARBY SIGHTS

San Antonio de Pala. Twenty-five miles to the east of San Luis Rey mission is its *asistencia* (sub-mission), San Antonio de Pala, located in the Pala Indian Reservation (3015 Pala Mission Road, Pala, California 92059). Fr. Peyri founded the asistencia on June 13, 1816, and named it in honor of St. Anthony of Padua, a renowned thirteenth-century Franciscan. Although many of the missions had asistencias associated with them, San Antonio de Pala is the only one still intact and continuing to serve its descendant Indian community.

The bell tower is freestanding, modeled after a tower in Ciudad Juarez. The two bells were cast in Mexico. At the top of the tower is a small cactus plant growing by the base of the cross. It's said that Fr. Peyri climbed the tower and planted a cactus to symbolize Christ conquering the desert—both the desert of California and the desert of the human heart. Behind the bell tower is the cemetery, containing the graves of mission neophytes and early settlers.

The simple chapel contains the original floor and interior walls decorated with murals by Indian artists. The crucifix was hand carved in the seventeenth century from Bestardo wood from the state of Michoacan in Mexico. The chapel offers a reflective and prayerful environment.

"Jewel of the Missions"
Founded November 1, 1776
26801 Ortega Highway
San Juan Capistrano, CA 92675
www.missionsjc.com

The charming ruins of the Great Stone Church
and the beautifully preserved structures of this
once-glorious "Jewel of the Missions," convey
a rich but tragic history. Fr. Junípero Serra founded it on All
Saints Day 1776 as the seventh of the California missions. San
Juan Capistrano flourished with a neophyte population of 1,361
at its peak. A main quadrangle encompassed a chapel, living
quarters, kitchen, workshops, storerooms, soldiers' barracks,
and other ancillary buildings, while the outlying fields yielded
abundant harvests of grains, corn, beans, peas, and lentils, and
livestock on the open range.

The natives of the region are the Acjachemen people. They
lived prosperously for thousands of years in small villages along
the coastlands. Fr. Geronimo Boscana, who was the resident
priest at Mission San Juan Capistrano from 1814 to 1826, has
written the earliest account of the customs and religion of the
Acjachemen.

The mission was actually founded twice. In 1775, the site had
been chosen, the cross set up, the bells rung, and the ground
dedicated. Then, after construction had been underway for
eight days, news arrived of the Indian attack on the San Diego
mission. The work stopped, the bells were hastily buried, and
the small group hurried to take shelter at the San Diego presidio.
The next year, when peace was assured, Fr. Serra found the cross

still in place, dug up the bells and hung them from a tree, and sang the founding ritual.

An adobe church, proudly known today as the Serra Chapel, was constructed in 1782. It is the oldest standing building in California and is today the only remaining California church in which St. Junípero Serra offered Mass. By 1796, this small adobe church became too small for the growing number of Indians at the mission, and work was begun on the Great Stone Church. But tragically, only six years after its completion, it was destroyed by the great earthquake of 1812.

In 1818, the mission was attacked by pirates. The French pirate Hipólito Bouchard sailed his two ships within sight of the mission and demanded provisions. The garrison of Spanish soldiers refused his request and threatened "an immediate supply of shot and shell" if the ships did not sail away. In response, Bouchard ordered an assault on the mission, sending 140 men with two or three light cannons to take the supplies by force. The mission guards engaged the attackers but were overwhelmed as the marauders looted the warehouses and left minor damages to the buildings in their wake.

The 1820s and 1830s saw a gradual decline in the mission's prosperity after Mexico gained its independence from Spain. Disease thinned out the once-ample cattle herds, and floods and droughts took their toll on the crops. But the biggest threat to the mission's stability came from the presence of Spanish settlers who sought to take over the mission's fertile lands after it was secularized. By 1842, the natives and Franciscans had left the mission, and it gradually decayed, as many of the tiles and timbers were plundered by the settlers. In 1865, President Lincoln returned the mission to the Church.

Fr. St. John O'Sullivan arrived in 1910 as the first resident priest in some twenty years, becoming rector in 1914. He spent many years working to restore the mission a section at a time, charging a ten-cent admission fee to help defray preservation costs. O'Sullivan died in 1933 and is buried in the mission cemetery at the foot of a Celtic cross.

The swallows of Capistrano are the most popular feature of the mission. These cliff swallows spend the summer on the grounds, building their nests of saliva and mud and protecting their young inside the ruins of the old stone church. A 1915 article in *Overland Monthly* magazine made note of the birds' annual habit of nesting beneath the eaves and archways of the mission. The mission's location near two rivers made it an ideal spot, as there was a constant supply of the insects on which they feed. Fr. O'Sullivan utilized public interest in the phenomenon to generate concern for the restoration efforts, and the swallows became the defining symbol of the mission.

The birds fly south to Argentina every year around October 23, the Feast of St. John of Capistrano, and return to nest at the mission near March 19, the Feast of St. Joseph. The song-writer Leon René was so inspired by this phenomenon that he composed the song "When the Swallows Come Back to Capistrano," which was performed by many artists in the coming decades. A glassed-off room in the mission honors René, displaying the upright piano on which he composed the tune, furniture from his office, and several copies of the song's sheet music. Each year the Fiesta de las Golondrinas (swallows) is held in the city of San Juan Capistrano, a week-long celebration culminating in the Swallows Day Parade and street fair.

PATRON OF THE MISSION

San Juan de Capistrano (St. John of Capistrano) was chosen by the Spanish viceroy and Fr. Serra as patron of the mission. As a Franciscan priest and powerful preacher, he attracted great throngs throughout Europe. He is also remembered, along with St. Bernardine of Siena, as a reformer of the Franciscan order.

John was born in the Italian town of Capistrano, Abruzzo, in 1386. He studied law at the University of Perugia and practiced as a lawyer in the courts of Naples. He was then appointed governor of Perugia in order to establish public order there. When war broke out between Perugia and the Malatesta family of Rimini in 1416, John was sent to broker a peace, but instead he was thrown in prison. During the captivity, he had a vision in which St. Francis of Assisi invited him to enter the Franciscan order. He made his religious profession in the order and became a student and follower of St. Bernardine of Siena.

After his ordination, John began his brilliant preaching apostolate, traveling throughout Italy, Germany, Bohemia, Austria, Hungary, Poland, and Russia. He was sent as a papal legate to resolve many disputes throughout Europe. At the age of seventy, John was commissioned by Pope Callistus III to preach and lead a crusade against the invading Turks, who were threatening Vienna and Rome. Marching at the head of seventy thousand Christians, he gained victory in the great battle of Belgrade in 1456. The city was saved and the enemy withdrew.

Three months later, he died at Ilok, Hungary (in today's Croatia), on October 23, which became his feast day. He was especially popular in the Austro-Hungarian Empire and is usually depicted wearing a Franciscan habit and a breastplate. Often he carries a sword and a red banner with the monogram of the Holy Name of Jesus, IHS, inspired by St. Bernardine. In addition to being patron of this mission, he is the patron of jurists. On the saint's tomb in the Austrian town of Villach, the governor had this message inscribed: "This tomb holds John, by birth of Capistrano, a man worthy of all praise, defender and promoter of the faith, guardian of the Church, herald of Christ, zealous protector of his order, an ornament to all the world, lover of truth and religious justice, mirror of life, surest guide in doctrine; praised by countless tongues, he reigns blessed in heaven."[51]

MISSION BELLS

To the right of the mission's main entrance is a campanario with four bells, which continue to be rung with hand-held ropes. When the Great Stone Church collapsed in the earthquake of 1812, the four surviving bells from the high tower were placed in this bell wall. The two largest bells were cracked and did not produce clear tones, so in 2000 they were taken down, used as molds, and replaced by duplicates.

Standing in front of the church ruins, a display with two large bells sits on the footprint of the original bell tower of the Great Stone Church. These are the original bells, cast in 1796. A close inspection shows their damage from the earthquake as well as the inscriptions dedicating them to San Vicente and San Juan.

MISSION CHURCH

All that remains of the Great Stone Church are its mellowed ruins located to the right of the main entrance to the mission. The standing masonry comprises only a small fragment of the original church, which was the largest and most beautiful of all the mission churches.

The church was designed in the shape of a cross, and the sandstone building sat on a foundation seven feet deep. Boulders and stones were quarried and hauled from up to six miles away, and construction continued for nine long years. The completed church was 180 feet long, and the walls were fifty-two feet in height. The tall bell tower soared above the church. Local legend has it that the tower could be seen for ten miles and that the bells could be heard from even farther away.

The church was finally completed in 1806. Its splendid dedication ceremony was followed by a three-day fiesta to celebrate the monumental event. But tragedy struck on the morning of December 8, 1812, when a series of large earthquakes shook all of southern California. The shaking racked the doors to the church, pinning them shut. Most of the nave came crashing down, and the bell tower was completely obliterated. Forty native worshipers who were attending Mass and two boys who had been ringing the bells in the tower were buried under the rubble and lost their lives.

Mass for the mission was offered thereafter in the older adobe chapel, which may be entered today from the section of the quadrangle closest to the bell wall and ruins. This lovely chapel is today dedicated to St. Junípero Serra because it is the only standing California church where the saint is known to have celebrated Mass.

The mission registers of baptisms, marriages, and burials are all intact and preserved, as is the confirmation register. These provide historical proof that Fr. Serra visited the mission in 1776, 1778, and 1783. He administered the sacrament of confirmation in October of 1783, less than a year before he died, confirming 221 individuals in this chapel.

The centerpiece of the chapel is its spectacular retablo that serves as the backdrop for the altar. A masterpiece of Baroque art, it was created in seventeenth-century Barcelona. The altarpiece was hand-carved from hundreds of individual pieces of mahogany and cedar, then overlaid in gold leaf. It was originally imported in 1806 for the Los Angeles cathedral but was never used. It was later donated to the mission and installed some-time between 1922 and 1924. The five figures in the niches are the following: St. John of Capistrano at the top, holding the red banner, St. Peter and St. Michael the Archangel on the upper left and right, and St. Francis of Assisi and St. Clare of Assisi on the lower left and right.

There is a prayer room within the chapel dedicated to St. Peregrine, the patron saint of those who suffer from cancer and other life-threatening diseases. The baptismal font near the entry was rescued from the Great Stone Church. Along the walls hang original eighteenth-century Stations of the Cross, and a painting of St. John of Capistrano from the eighteenth century hangs above one of the side doors.

This ancient and beloved Serra Chapel is still a place of quiet prayer for those who visit the mission and a tangible memory of the holy saint. It remains in active use today, often the site of Catholic Masses, weddings, baptisms, and funerals.

—PRAYER—

We adore You, Lord Jesus Christ, here, and in all your churches throughout the whole world, and we bless You, because by your holy Cross, You have redeemed the world (St. Francis of Assisi).

A READING FROM THE SECOND LETTER OF ST. PAUL TO THE CORINTHIANS:

Brothers and sisters, the love of Christ urges us on, because we are convinced that one has died for all; therefore all have died. And he died for all, so that those who live might live no longer for themselves, but for him who died and was raised for them.

From now on, therefore, we regard no one from a human point of view; even though we once knew Christ from a human point of view, we know him no longer in that way. So if anyone is in Christ, there is a new creation: everything old has passed away; see, everything has become new! All this is from God, who reconciled us to himself through Christ, and has given us the ministry of reconciliation; that is, in Christ God was reconciling the world to himself, not counting their trespasses against them, and entrusting the message of reconciliation to us. So we are ambassadors for Christ, since God is making his appeal through us; we entreat you on behalf of Christ, be reconciled to God (2 Corinthians 5:14–20).

V: St. John of Capistrano, Franciscan reformer and preacher of the Gospel,

R: Inspire us to be missionary disciples.

V: St. John of Capistrano, holding high the standard of the holy name of Jesus as our sign of victory and life,

R: Inspire us to be missionary disciples.

V: St. Junípero Serra, apostle to North America and model of simplicity,

R: Inspire us to be missionary disciples.

V: St. Junípero Serra, dedicated evangelizer of the native peoples in California,

R: Inspire us to be missionary disciples.

Let us pray:

O God, by whose grace St. John of Capistrano and St. Junípero Serra persevered in proclaiming the Gospel of your Son, Jesus Christ, grant us through their inspiration and intercession that we may faithfully walk in our own vocation. Make us ambassadors for Christ and missionary disciples in our world today. Amen.

MUSEUM AND GROUNDS

The grounds of the mission are a treasury of archaeological findings and historical artifacts. The soldiers' barracks contain exhibits that detail the life of the troops stationed at the mission, and the padres' rooms highlight the simple, rustic existence of the missionaries. The Native American room is dedicated to the culture of the Acjachemen people. The Mission Treasures features rare paintings, historical objects, and sacred religious pieces.

The wine vat in one of the museum rooms recalls the fact that the California wine industry began here. The first vineyard was located on these grounds, with the planting of the Criollo or "mission grape" in 1779. The mission winery, built in 1783, is where the first wine of California was produced—red and white wines (sweet and dry), brandy, and a port-like fortified wine called Angelica, all from the single grape. The brick-lined crushing vat is inside the museum and the fermentation vat is outside the wall.

The cereal grains of wheat and barley, grown in the mission fields, were dried and ground by stone into flour, while large bodegas (warehouses) provided long-term storage for all the products manufactured at the mission. The preserved foodstuffs were used to prepare and serve thousands of meals every day from the mission's kitchens and bakeries.

The mission industrial center displays large tallow vats, source of an important industry for the mission. Animal fat from sheep and cattle was melted down in large kettles to make tallow, which was then used to make candles, soap, grease, and ointments. Also situated in this area were looms for weaving, vats for dyeing wool cloth, and areas for tanning leather. Cow hides were cleaned, dried, soaked in lime water to loosen the hair, then scraped, beaten for softening, and soaked in tanning solution for several months. The hides were then stretched and beaten with tallow to soften them and then hung to dry. The hides became the most important trade item for the mission.

By the 1830s, when the missions were secularized, little of the mission's assets remained, but the manufacture of hides and tallow continued full swing. This brisk international trade is described in Richard Henry Dana's classic novel, *Two Years Before the Mast.*

The central courtyard with its fountain and gardens is a good place to relax and contemplate the lives of all the Native Americans, Franciscan padres, Spaniards, and generous restorers who have made the mission the jewel that it is today. The audio guide provides information and colorful recollections of life at the mission during the modern period of restoration.

OTHER NEARBY SIGHTS

Mission Basilica San Juan Capistrano. Outside the mission walls, but just around the corner, is the modern Mission Basilica San Juan Capistrano. Its terracotta-colored dome and bell tower can be seen from the mission grounds. The 85-foot-high main rotunda and 104-foot bell tower make it the tallest building in the town. The basilica was opened on the Feast of San Juan Capistrano in 1986 and dedicated in February of 1987. Pope John Paul II designated the church as a minor basilica in 2000, and it was declared a national shrine in 2003. Both as a basilica and a national shrine, the church is an officially sanctioned and recommended place of pilgrimage.

The design of the modern church is patterned after the mission's original Great Stone Church that today stands in ruins. The motifs on the interior walls were designed and painted by Norman Neuerberg. A prominent feature of the basilica is the "Grand Retablo," a 42-foot-high altar-backing carved in Brazilian cedar and covered in gold leaf. It is stylistically reminiscent of the retablo in the Serra Chapel of the mission and the other Spanish colonial retablos. It was constructed in Madrid,

Spain, by 85 artisans under the direction of Juan Antonio Medina. It was created throughout 2006, and by March 19, 2007, the team had assembled the masterpiece for Mass on the Feast of St. Joseph. The central image of the retablo is the crucified Christ being received by God the Father. An image of Our Lady of Guadalupe fills the shrine below. To the side of these figures are shrines to four saints: St. Junípero Serra and St. Kateri Tekakwitha above, St. Joseph and St. Francis below. Each of these shrines is ornamented on each side by a pair of solomonic columns, decorated in relief with the mission's twisting grape vines and its legendary swallows.

Christ Cathedral. The contemporary Christ Cathedral, in Garden Grove, is on the route north toward Los Angeles. The reflective glass building, designed by American architect Philip Johnson, was completed in 1981 for the ministry of Robert Schuller. In recent years, it has been redesigned and consecrated as the cathedral for the Catholic Diocese of Orange.

"The Pride of the Missions"

Founded on September 8, 1771

428 S. Mission Drive

San Gabriel, CA 91776

www.sangabrielmissionchurch.org

Named for God's heavenly messenger, Mission San Gabriel was the fourth mission founded in the mission chain. Junípero Serra appointed two priests, Fr. Cambon and Fr. Somera, to begin the mission, and it was the first mission established without Serra's actual presence. Those early days were marked with both wonder and tragedy.

According to Fr. Palóu in his biography of Serra, as the founding expedition was deliberating over the exact site for the mission, they were confronted by a large crowd of the native Tongva people, whose intention was to drive the strangers away from their land. But as the Indians brandished their weapons, one of the padres held up a canvas painting of Our Lady of Sorrows. These Gabrieliños, as they were later designated by the Spaniards, were so struck by the beauty of the woman that they offered signs of friendship to the missionaries. This three hundred–year-old work of art can be seen today in the mission church.

However, as the new mission was being constructed with the willing help of the Indians, a soldier assigned to the mission assaulted the wife of one of the native chieftains. Seeking to avenge the wrong, the chief (and a band of natives) charged the culprit, but was himself killed in the skirmish. The corporal of the soldiers ordered that the head of the chief be cut off and impaled on a pole to warn against further aggression. Although no further attacks were made, it was a long time before the Indians trusted the missionaries, and conversions were slow in coming. Sadly, this deplorable deed was only one of a long series of what Serra called "most heinous crimes" committed by the troops.

When the two founding missionaries requested transfer because of the unchecked abuse they had witnessed, Serra sent Fr. Cruzado and Fr. Paterna. Although the hatred of the Indians for the military did not diminish, the patience and gentleness of the padres enabled them to gradually gain the confidence of the natives. In time, a few children were presented for baptism. In fact, the first child to be offered was the son of the slain Indian chief, a peace offering by his widow that helped to soften mistrust among the natives.

In 1772, Serra was traveling southward, picking out future mission sites, and was able to visit San Gabriel for the first time. He was delighted with the location and the progress it was making, declaring it "without doubt the most excellent mission site so far discovered." With prophetic insights, he stated, "Once it is sufficiently developed, it will be able, doubtless, to sustain not only itself, but all the rest." He was very pleased with the seven or eight Indian orphans the friars had taken in: "precious creatures, one of whom spoke Spanish beautifully."[52]

The frequent flooding of the river and the resultant loss of crops forced the padres in 1775 to move the mission to its present location. In that same year, Fr. Paterna was moved from the mission, and Fr. Sanchez took his place to work alongside Fr. Cruzado for nearly thirty years. Well more than 25,000 baptisms were conducted at San Gabriel between 1771 and 1834, making it the most spiritually fertile of all the missions. In its heyday, it furnished food and supplies to settlements and other missions throughout California, just as Serra had prophesied. The Indians became skilled at weaving and leather-work, and the mission became famous for its fine wines.

A new church made of brick and mortar was begun in 1779. After twenty-six years of building it, the two faithful padres died in 1805, the year the church was complete, and Fr. Zalvidea carried on the work of the mission for the next twenty years. With great physical strength, heroic faith, and tireless dedication, he led the mission to its greatest prosperity. By 1834, the mission inventory included: 160,000 grapevines in four vine-yards, more than 2,300 fruit trees in nine orchards, and 22,000 heads of livestock.

At that time, the secularization laws required the Franciscans to turn over all of the mission's vast wealth. The 1,323 Christian Indians scattered, as the property, which was supposed to be their inheritance from the Franciscans, fell under the adminis-tration of Governor Pio Pico. The mission and its surroundings quickly fell into ruins. In 1859, President Buchanan restored the church to the Catholic diocese, and it was a parish church for the city of San Gabriel from 1862 until 1908, when the Claretian Missionary Fathers came to San Gabriel and began the job of rebuilding and restoring the site.

PATRON OF THE MISSION

San Gabriel Arcángel (St. Gabriel the Archangel) is one of three angels mentioned by name in the Bible. Gabriel appears first in the book of Daniel, interpreting Daniel's visions and revealing the messianic times. In the Gospel of Luke, Gabriel is the bearer of good tidings to God's people. He is identified as "the angel of the Lord" who announces the birth of John the Baptist to Zechariah and the birth of Jesus to Mary. Gabriel is also known to Muslims, who believe him to be the angel who served as the mouthpiece of God in dictating the Qu'ran to Mohammed.

San Gabriel has been depicted as a winged messenger of God from the time of ancient Christianity. He is most often drawn, painted, or sculpted in the context of the Annunciation to Mary. San Gabriel mission—like the elderly Zechariah and Elizabeth and the Virgin Mary in Nazareth—became an instrument of God's work in the world, bringing salvation to all on whom God's favor rests.

MISSION BELLS

The brick and mortar church experienced heavy damage in the earthquake of 1812, and the bell tower, which at the time was at the front of the church, was toppled. By 1828, the church was completely restored. The bell tower was replaced by a campanario, erected at the other end of the church, where three rows of arched openings now hold six bells, dating from 1795 to the 1830s.

The oldest bells were cast in Mexico City by the famous bell maker Paul Ruelas. The largest bell rang the Angelus over the countryside for over a century. Weighing at least a ton, its clear tone could be heard in the growing town of Los Angeles, eight miles away.

MISSION CHURCH

The church, built of stone, brick, and mortar, has been well-preserved since its completion in 1805. Its strength is due to the basic, but effective, engineering skills of the early builders. The unique exterior—with a Moorish style designed by Fr. Cruzado—resembles the cathedral and former mosque of Córdoba, Spain, where the priest received his early education. Its fortress-like appearance, featuring picturesque capped buttresses and lofty walls with narrow windows, is unique among the mission churches.

The floors and walls inside the church are original. The baptistery features a domed roof and holds the hammered copper baptismal font, which was a personal gift from King Carlos III of Spain. It also contains the original sterling silver baptismal shell carried by the founding fathers. The silver shell pours the waters of baptism over children today just as it did over the first Tongva child in 1771.

The reredos was handcrafted in Mexico City and brought to the Mission in the 1790s. The six polychrome wooden statues, with the winged San Gabriel Arcángel at the top, were hand carved in Spain and brought here in 1791. The other statues are St. Francis and St. Anthony of Padua, on the top left and right, and St. Joachim (the husband of St. Anne and father of Mary), the Immaculate Conception, and St. Dominic, from left to right at the bottom.

The ancient painting of Our Lady of Sorrows, which so fascinated the Tongva at the mission's founding, is now nicely framed with wrought iron in the shape of a cross. The inscriptions in the floor mark the burial place of several of the Franciscans who served the mission, including Fr. Miguel Sanchez and Fr. Antonio Cruzado.

The fourteen Stations of the Cross are some of the missions' most exceptional Native American artwork, mixing indigenous and imported artistic traditions. Olive oil was used as the base and the pigments came from wild flowers. In these wonderful images, Christ appears as an Indian, as do Veronica, soothing his face with a cloth, and Simon of Cyrene, helping Christ carry his cross. The Roman soldiers have an uncanny resemblance to the Spanish military.

—PRAYER—

We adore You, Lord Jesus Christ, here, and in all your churches throughout the whole world, and we bless You, because by your holy Cross, You have redeemed the world (St. Francis of Assisi).

A READING FROM THE GOSPEL ACCORDING TO ST. LUKE:
In the sixth month the angel Gabriel was sent by God to a town in Galilee called Nazareth, to a virgin engaged to a man whose name was Joseph, of the house of David. The virgin's name was Mary. And he came to her and said, "Greetings, favored one! The Lord is with you." But she was much perplexed by his words and pondered what sort of greeting this might be. The angel said to her, "Do not be afraid, Mary, for you have found favor with God. And now, you will conceive in your womb and bear a son, and you will name him Jesus. He will be great, and will be called the Son of the Most High, and the Lord God will give to him the throne of his ancestor David. He will reign over the house of Jacob forever, and of his kingdom there will be no end." Mary said to the angel, "How can this be, since I am a virgin?" The angel said to her, "The Holy Spirit will come upon you, and the power of the Most High will overshadow you; therefore the child to be born will be holy; he will be called Son of God. And now, your relative Elizabeth in her old age has also conceived a son; and this is the sixth month for her who was said to be barren. For nothing will be impossible with God." Then Mary said, "Here am I, the servant of the Lord; let it be with me according to your word." Then the angel departed from her (Luke 1:26–38).

V: St. Gabriel, holy archangel who stands before the throne of God,

R: Pray for us.

V: St. Gabriel, herald of the Incarnation and guardian of the Immaculate Virgin,

R: Pray for us.

V: St. Gabriel, who proclaimed Jesus as the Son of the Most High who will reign over God's kingdom forever,

R: Pray for us.

V: St. Gabriel, defender of the faith, strength of the just, and protector of the faithful,

R: Pray for us.

Let us pray:

O God, who first announced the Good News of Jesus Christ to Mary through the message of your angel, help us listen to your Gospel and take it to heart. Through the intercession of your archangel Gabriel, help us receive the redemption obtained for us by your Son, so that we may sing your praises forever with your angels in the land of the living. Amen.

MUSEUM AND GROUNDS

The grounds are lovely, and the original buildings have been brought back to life. Behind the altar wall of the church is the sacristy, the best preserved in all the missions. Its walls, floor, and vaulted ceilings are all original. The chest of drawers, mirror, and frame are also original and completely made without nails. Beside the church stands the *campo santo* (cemetery), consecrated in 1778. The large crucifix is a memorial to the six thousand Gabrielino Indians who died over the years of the mission's operation.

The adobe mission building from 1812, which once housed a weaving room, carpentry shops, and storage rooms for grains, now houses the museum. Displays include original art, photography, baskets, liturgical vestments, Bibles, a baptismal record, and priceless books dating to 1489. Other artifacts include a rosewood organ from France and a Spanish bedroom dated to 1623. Another building contains the original winery, where the grapes were crushed, the juice was fermented in vats, and the wine was aged in barrels. Olive oil was also processed here.

On the patio where the statue of St. Junípero Serra stands,

the baked floor tiles, bases of pillars, and water cistern are original. The grapevine and olive trees were planted in the eighteenth and nineteenth centuries. In another section of the quadrangle stands the aqueduct, which was fed from a nearby stream with underground clay pipes. The aqueduct then supplied water to the kitchen, laundry, and tannery, and it irrigated the fields, orchards, and vineyards. The five fire circles held large kettles for cooking *pozole* (hominy stew), the daily lunch at the mission. After the sounding of the noontime bell and the praying of the Angelus, the Indians came to the mission to be fed. The reconstructed kitchen, with its oven and other artifacts, is typical of those used in the missions.

Beyond the cactus garden are four enormous boilers for rendering tallow, used for making soap and candles. The nearby Peace Garden includes the anchor from a topsail schooner, the *Guadalupe*, which was built at the mission in 1930. The first ship constructed in California, she sailed the coast of Mexico, delivering goods from the mission. The mission blacksmiths cut off and melted pieces of the anchor to make hinges, hoes, and other tools. The garden also contains a tile image of Our Lady of Guadalupe. A bench and flowers make it a lovely spot for meditation and prayer.

OTHER NEARBY SIGHTS
San Gabriel Civic Auditorium. Around the corner from the mission, the Mission Playhouse, now the San Gabriel Civic Auditorium, was built by John Steven McGroaty to present his epic Mission Play. Beginning in 1912, the play told the story of the California missions and drew people from all over the world to San Gabriel.

The Playhouse was planned and completed for the 1927 season, with stage and dressing rooms large enough to accommodate the cast of 150 for the four-and-a-half-hour production. The exterior is patterned after Mission San Antonio de Padua, and the interior decor is a blend of Spanish, Indian, and Mexican influences. In the courtyard are replicas of all twenty-one missions. McGroaty served for two terms in Congress and was Poet Laureate of California from 1933 until his death in 1944.

Our Lady Queen of the Angels. El Pueblo de Nuestra Señora la Reina de los Ángeles (the Town of Our Lady Queen of the Angels) was founded in 1781 when eleven families, escorted by a company of soldiers, departed Mission San Gabriel to establish the new town. The civilian pueblo became the principal urban center of southern California and by the twentieth century became the American metropolis of Los Angeles. The name derives from Santa Maria degli Angeli (St. Mary of the Angels), the chapel outside of Assisi that St. Francis made the heart of the Franciscan order, calling it La Porciúncula. The river that the early explorers called El Río Porciúncula is today's Los Angeles River.

The historical district is clustered around Los Angeles Plaza. La Iglesia de Nuestra Señora la Reina de Los Ángeles (The Church of Our Lady the Queen of the Angels) was founded in 1814 and dedicated in 1822. The present church, built from materials of the original church, dates from 1861. Sometimes called La Placita (The Plaza Church), it is a parish church of the Archdiocese of Los Angeles.

Cathedral of Our Lady of the Angels. Opened in 2002, the contemporary cathedral is the mother church of the Archdiocese of Los Angeles. It contains many works of art, including the twenty-five tapestries of the Communion of Saints, created by artist John Nava. The work depicts 135 saints and blesseds from around the world, and twelve untitled figures, including children of all ages, represent the many anonymous holy people in our midst. All of the figures direct the worshipers to the great Cross window above the altar.

"Mission of the Valley"

Founded on September 8, 1797

15151 San Fernando Mission Boulevard

Mission Hills, CA 91345

www.archivalcenter.org

This mission was founded in the spacious area that later came to be called San Fernando Valley. The early explorers had noted the location as ideal for a future mission because of its four flowing streams and friendly Indians. The native population was made up of the Tongva and Chumash peoples, some of whom had already experienced Europeans through contact with the growing pueblo of Los Angeles. This "Mission of the Valley" was founded on September 8, 1797, by Fr. Fermín Lasuén, then the Father-President of the California missions. San Fernando Rey de España was the seventeenth of the "ladder" of missions envisioned by St. Junípero Serra.

A small chapel was raised within the first two months, and soon a granary, storeroom, and weaving room were in operation. A year later, a new church had to be built to accommodate the mission's growing population. Seven years after its founding, there were more than a thousand neophytes being housed on the property. By then, all of the buildings were tile-roofed, and the quadrangle was surrounded by barracks, workshops, and storerooms.

In 1806, a new adobe church was completed and dedicated. Among the dedication festivities, musical bands of Indians came with their instruments from other missions and presented a concert of music and songs they had learned in the mission choirs. The 1812 earthquake inflicted extensive damage, and new beams and buttresses were installed for support.

At its peak in 1819, the mission had more than 30,000 grape-vines, a wine factory, and more than 1,000 fruit trees. In addition, it had more than 12,000 head of cattle and maintained a large trade in hides and tallow. Developing skills in leather-working, the Indians made shoes, clothes, and saddles for their own use and for trading.

In the years following 1834, when the land was administered by the Mexican government, the roof tiles and anything else of value were removed by settlers for use on their own property. In 1842, six years before the California Gold Rush, Francisco Lopez took a rest under an oak tree on one of the mission ranches and, as the story goes, had a dream that he was floating on a pool of gold. When he awoke, he pulled a few wild onions from the ground and found flakes of gold in the roots. The Lopez gold find, under the "Oak of the Golden Dream," as it is known today, was the first documented discovery of gold in California. This sparked a gold rush—though on a much smaller scale than the Gold Rush of 1848—in which about two thousand people, mostly from the Mexican state of Sonora, came to Rancho San Francisco to mine for gold. Over the next four years, they dug up everything that could be dug up, including the floor of the mission church, under the assumption that the padres had hidden a store of gold there.

Many attempts were made in the early twentieth century to restore the old mission, but it was not until the Hearst Foundation gave a large gift of money in the 1940s that the Mission was finally restored. Today the mission is operated by the Archdiocese of Los Angeles.

PATRON OF THE MISSION

San Fernando Rey de España (St. Ferdinand King of Spain), a member of the Third Order of St. Francis, ruled in the thirteenth century. He is also the patron of the Franciscan missionary college in Mexico City, where Serra and the other missionaries were trained to work among the indigenous populations of New Spain and from where they were sent to California. Because these Franciscans were under the jurisdiction of the College of San Fernando, they became known as Fernandinos.

Born in Salamanca, Ferdinand was the son of King Alfonso IX of Leon and Berengaria, daughter of King Alphonso III of Castile. He became King of Castile in 1217 and succeeded to the crown of Leon in 1230, uniting the kingdoms of Castile and Leon. Ferdinand was an outstanding ruler and a man of deep Christian faith. He ruled with great compassion for his subjects and avoided overburdening them with taxation. He founded and endowed hospitals, bishoprics, monasteries, and churches during his reign.

King Ferdinand waged successful campaigns against the forces of Islam, eventually expelling the Moors from most of Spain. He conquered Cordoba and Seville and transformed their great mosques into cathedrals. He is also remembered for his reform of Spanish law, the code of which was used until the modern era, and for founding the University of Salamanca.

After a prolonged illness, he died on May 30, 1252. He desired to be buried in the simple habit of his secular Franciscan order. St. Fernando is usually depicted in statues and paintings crowned as a king and wearing a breastplate beneath his royal robes. He often holds either a scepter or a sword and also an orb topped with a cross.

His heroic life is joined to the image of La Virgen de los Reyes (The Virgin of the Kings), to whom he attributed his rule and victories. One story says that the king saw the Virgin in a dream, and the next day he called the master carvers to create a wooden image equal to his vision in the night. Another story holds that the statue was a gift from Ferdinand's cousin, Louis IX of France. In fact, the image accompanied King Ferdinand in his battles and came to Seville in 1248, presiding over the army's triumphal entry into the city.

St. Ferninand was canonized in 1671, and his remains are preserved in the Cathedral of Seville at the altar of the Royal Chapel. Enthroned above his tomb is La Virgen de los Reyes, the patroness of the city. Each year she is dressed in royal garments and processed through the streets on the Feast of Mary's Assumption on August 15.

MISSION BELLS

A plain two-story square bell tower to the right of the church entrance has held up to four bells in its history. One of these bells, which hung for many years in the portico of the court-yard, was returned in 2013 to Holy Resurrection Cathedral in Kodiak, Alaska, the oldest Orthodox parish in North America.

The bell, by its shape, design, decoration, and sound is clearly a Russian bell cast in Alaska in 1796. How it came into the possession of the San Fernando mission is a mystery, but perhaps it was a goodwill gift made by the Russian colonists in Alaska in initiating trade with California. The return of the bell was a gesture of friendship between the native Catholics of California and the native Orthodox of Alaska. A replica of the bell was given to the mission by the Orthodox Church and now hangs in the courtyard portico.

MISSION CHURCH

The San Fernando earthquake of 1971 damaged the church, which had to be demolished and completely rebuilt. The new church, completed in 1974, is an exact replica of the church of 1806. The walls are seven feet thick at the base, tapering to five feet at the top. The walls, niches, and arches are painted in muted shades of red and blue against a white background.

The elaborate altar and reredos are carved from walnut and date to 1687. They were originally in a chapel in Spain and installed here in 1991. The central image is San Fernando, King of Spain, with representations of the Trinity surrounding him. The dove symbolizing the Holy Spirit is at the top, with the Son and the Father to the left and right, and a golden sunburst illumining the scene. The images above to the left and right are St. Philip Neri and St. Dominic. The images in the frames to the left and right below are St. Mary Magdalene and St. Junípero Serra. In the middle, above the tabernacle, is a statue of Nuestra Señora del Pilar, the patroness of Spain.

—PRAYER—

We adore You, Lord Jesus Christ, here, and in all your churches throughout the whole world, and we bless You, because by your holy Cross, You have redeemed the world (St. Francis of Assisi).

A READING FROM THE GOSPEL ACCORDING TO ST. LUKE:
And Mary said, "My soul magnifies the Lord, and my spirit rejoices in God my Savior, for he has looked with favor on the lowliness of his servant. Surely, from now on all generations will call me blessed; for the Mighty One has done great things for me, and holy is his name. His mercy is for those who fear him from generation to generation. He has shown strength with his arm; he has scattered the proud in the thoughts of their hearts. He has brought down the powerful from their thrones, and lifted up the lowly; he has filled the hungry with good things, and sent the rich away empty. He has helped his servant Israel,

in remembrance of his mercy, according to the promise he made to our ancestors, to Abraham and to his descendants forever" (Luke 1:46–55).

V: Mary, most wise, powerful, and merciful,

R: Holy Mary, Mother of God, pray for us sinners, now and at the hour of our death.

V: Daughter of the Father, Mother of the Son, and Spouse of the Holy Spirit,

R: Holy Mary, Mother of God, pray for us sinners, now and at the hour of our death.

V: Virgin of the Kings and Queen of Heaven,

R: Holy Mary, Mother of God, pray for us sinners, now and at the hour of our death.

V: Mother of the Word of God and Star of the New Evangelization,

R: Holy Mary, Mother of God, pray for us sinners, now and at the hour of our death.

Let us pray:

O God, who looked on the lowliness of the Blessed Virgin Mary and crowned her with surpassing glory, we praise you for the radiant gift of our mother in heaven. As the beginning and image of your Church coming to perfection, may she be a sure sign of hope for your pilgrim people. Grant that, under her protection and loving intercession, we may overcome sin and enter the joys of your kingdom forever. Amen.

MUSEUM AND GROUNDS

The museum offers an extensive showcase of beadwork, pottery, basketry, and other crafts made by the Indians at the mission. In addition, exhibits show a collection of miniature mission bells, liturgical vestments, *santos* (religious images), and remembrances of the visit of Pope St. John Paul II to the mission in

1987. The photographs offer a pictorial history of the mission, showing the neglect and disintegration it underwent following secularization. The images form a strong contrast to the impressive reconstruction seen today. The reconstructed house of the *mayordomo* (foreman of the mission) shows a dining room, beds, and housewares from the period.

The large *convento*, sometimes called the "long building," is the only building still standing from the days of the mission. Its roadside front features a colonnade of twenty-one arches. It presents refurbished rooms with authentic furnishings, including a room prepared for Bishop Francisco Garcia Diego, the first bishop of California. The wine cellar has been preserved, showing how wine was kept cool and dark as it was stored in wooden casks beneath the building. The convento also displays one of the oldest libraries in California, holding more than six hundred volumes from the mission era and before. At the far end of the building, with a separate entrance, is the Madonna Room, containing paintings, statues, and other depictions of the Blessed Mother.

The lovely East and West Gardens feature rare trees and beautiful flowers, along with a flower-shaped fountain, grinding stone, wine vat, and a statue of Fr. Fermín Lasuén in an ivy-hung niche. As successor to Fr. Serra as Father-President of the California missions, Fr. Lasuén founded nine missions, including this one. On the other side of the church, the cemetery encloses a memorial to the 2,425 Native Americans buried here. And further on, the Memorial Garden holds the earthly remains of the comedian Bob Hope and his wife Delores DeFina Hope.

To the right of the church, in an extension of the museum, a series of workshops illustrate the various industries at which the neophytes worked within the mission. The carpentry, pottery, saddles, blacksmith, and weaving shops recreate mission life with authentic furnishings. Finally, the Archival Center, operated by the Archdiocese of Los Angeles, collects, restores, catalogues, and displays manuscripts, documents, diaries, and photographs of California history in order to make them available to researchers. The task of preserving history is ongoing and essential for the future.

OTHER NEARBY SIGHTS

Brand Park. With its Memory Garden, Brand Park is located directly across the street from the mission. The garden contains one of the mission's original fountains, as well as tallow pits and soap vats, also remnants of the mission. Next to the fountain is a lovely statue of St. Junípero Serra guiding a young Indian boy. The park has picnic facilities for relaxing.

Andres Pico Adobe Park. The second-oldest adobe house in Los Angeles, Andres Pico Adobe Park stands about four blocks from the park and mission. The oldest part was built by the mission Indians, but later it was the home of the ranchero who owned the entire San Fernando Valley. The adobe itself is managed by the San Fernando Valley Historical Society, which restored the interior to demonstrate rancho life in nineteenth-century California.

"Mission by the Sea"

Founded on March 31, 1782

211 East Main Street

Ventura, CA 93001

www.sanbuenaventuramission.org

This ninth mission, and the last of the missions founded by St. Junípero Serra, lies midway between the missions at San Diego and Monterey, the first and second missions founded by the venerable Franciscan. Serra's original plan was to found this mission to St. Bonaventure as the third mission in the chain, but uprisings and political negotiations over use of the land delayed the founding for twelve years.

This "Mission by the Sea" was the first mission along the Santa Bárbara Channel, a waterway between the mainland of California and a series of islands off the coast. The area was home to the Chumash peoples—estimated by explorers to be no fewer than twenty thousand—who lived in dozens of villages near the shore and on the islands. The Chumash were described as friendly, artistic, and industrious. They wove beautiful baskets so tightly that they held water, and they navigated the waterways in finely fashioned plank canoes. Always his favorites, Serra described them as charming and attractive, waiting silently for the Gospel.

In a great procession, the founding expedition set out from Mission San Gabriel. Pack animals were loaded with church goods, furnishings, and tools for tilling the soil. On Easter morning, March 31, 1782, a cross was raised on the beach of the Santa Bárbara Channel, near the Chumash village of

Mitsqanaqa'n with about five hundred inhabitants. Fr. Serra celebrated the Mass, assisted by Fr. Pedro Benito Cambon, and preached on the resurrection.

The aging Serra left the mission to be administered by Fr. Cambon. Under his direction, the Chumash built a system of aqueducts that ran from the Ventura River to holding tanks at the mission, a total of about seven miles. This influx of water allowed a wide variety of crops to grow, including orchards, gardens, fruits, vegetables, grains, and even exotic crops such as bananas, coconuts, and figs. English navigator George Vancouver described the gardens as the finest he had seen.

The original church building was destroyed by fire within ten years. The present church was begun in 1792 and was completed, along with the quadrangle, in 1809. But the earthquake of 1812 and its accompanying tidal wave was so severe that the padres and native neophytes were forced to find temporary shelter a few miles inland. After repairs were made, the mission had to be abandoned again in 1818, when the Argentine pirate Bouchard was spotted offshore. The padres assembled the silver, statues, paintings, and vestments, hiding some in a cave and burying others. Then, with baskets of food, they moved livestock up into the hills for a month until Bouchard passed by.

After the secularization decree divested the padres of administrative control over the mission, the mission was rented to two Californios in 1845, then illegally sold by governor Pio Pico. The deal was voided by the Americans after they acquired California, and the mission was returned to the Church with the signature of President Abraham Lincoln in 1862. In 1893, Fr. Cyprian Rubio "modernized" the church interior, painting over the original artwork, lengthening the windows, and covering the beamed ceiling and tile floors.

Restoration work, carried out under the direction of Fr. Aubrey O'Reilly, began in 1956. The original floor and ceilings were uncovered and repaired, and the windows were reconstructed to their original size. Much of the artwork has since been restored to its original beauty. The mission now looks much like it did in its prime.

PATRON OF THE MISSION

San Buenaventura (St. Bonaventure) was born Giovanni de Fidanza in the village of Bagnoregio in Tuscany in 1221. According to legend, he received the name Bonaventure at the age of four when Francis of Assisi prayed for him due to an illness and exclaimed "O! Buona ventura (O! Good Fortune) for God's abiding grace." He took his degree at the Sorbonne in Paris at the same time as the Dominican St. Thomas Aquinas. He entered the Franciscan order in 1238 at the age of seventeen.

One of the finest minds of his age, Bonaventure was an outstanding philosopher and theologian. He was elected minister general of the Franciscan order and did much to reform the community. In 1273 he became cardinal bishop of Albano and aided Pope Gregory X in organizing the Council of Lyons to discuss the reunion of the Eastern and Western Churches. St. Bonaventure was canonized in 1482 and declared a Doctor of the Church in 1588.

The saint is usually depicted wearing a Franciscan habit, sometimes with a surplice and the scarlet cloak of a cardinal. He is often shown with a book and a pen, and is sometimes carrying a model of a church. His image, in statues and paintings, is found in several of the mission churches and museums.

MISSION BELLS

The campanile contains five bells in two tiers. The bell facing north is labeled "San Francisco 1781," the bell facing east has the inscription "San Pedro Alcantra 1781," and the bell facing south is topped with a crown and is inscribed, "Ave Maria Pruysyma D Sapoyan Ano D 1825," which means "Hail Immaculate Mary of Zapopan Year of the Lord 1825." The bell in the top arch was cast in Paris, France, in 1956 and is inscribed "Ave Maria S. Joseph."

The museum contains two wooden bells, carved out of two-foot blocks of wood. These curious items are the only two wooden bells found at the missions. Some assume that they were used during Holy Week when the metal bells were normally silent, but the bells were made with a metal band inside for the clapper to strike. Their use remains a mystery.

MISSION CHURCH

The main altar and its reredos originated in Mexico and was installed when the church was dedicated in 1809. The central figure is St. Bonaventure, and to the left and right are Mary the Immaculate Conception and St. Joseph holding the Christ child.

To the left of the main altar is the shrine of the crucifixion. The corpus of the crucifix originated in the Philippines and is believed to be more than four hundred years old. The scene includes the Sorrowful Mother of Jesus on the left and St. John, the Beloved Disciple, on the right. Higher up are figures of St. Anthony of Padua on the left and St. Thomas Aquinas on the right.

To the right of the main altar is a 250-year-old painting of Our Lady of Guadalupe from 1747 created by Francisco Cabrere. To the left and right are statues of St. Gertrude and St. Isidore. Smaller statues to the left and right are of St. Dominic and St. Francis.

Carpet was removed from the sanctuary in 2011, revealing the original floor tiles. The high walls are painted in hues of pink and mauve, with frescoed flowers in pink and green separating the painted columns. The Stations of the Cross are from the original church. From the beams of the ceiling are hung wooden chandeliers.

The baptistery contains original articles used for liturgical worship: chalices, ciborium, crucifixes, missal stands, monstrances, an aspergillum, containers for holy oils, and various relics. The hammered copper baptismal font is likely the work of a Chumash metalworker.

—PRAYER—

We adore You, Lord Jesus Christ, here, and in all your churches throughout the whole world, and we bless You, because by your holy Cross, You have redeemed the world (St. Francis of Assisi).

A READING FROM ST. PAUL'S LETTER TO THE EPHESIANS:
For this reason I bow my knees before the Father, from whom every family in heaven and on earth takes its name. I pray that, according to the riches of his glory, he may grant that you may be strengthened in your inner being with power through his Spirit, and that Christ may dwell in your hearts through faith, as you are being rooted and grounded in love. I pray that you may have the power to comprehend, with all the saints, what is the breadth and length and height and depth, and to know the love of Christ that surpasses knowledge, so that you may be filled with all the fullness of God (Ephesians 3:14–19).

V: St. Bonaventure, who sought the breadth and length and height and depth to know the love of Christ,

R: Pray for us.

V: St. Bonaventure, teacher and second founder of the Seraphic order of St. Francis,

R: Pray for us.

V: St. Bonaventure, Cardinal and Doctor of the Church, who embraced mortification and great humiliation,

R: Pray for us.

V: St. Bonaventure, whose mind was filled with learning and whose heart overflowed with charity,

R: Pray for us.

Let us pray in the words of St. Bonaventure for the Gifts of the Holy Spirit:

We beg the all-merciful Father through thee, his only-begotten Son made man for our sake, crucified and glorified for us, to send upon us from his treasure-house the Spirit of sevenfold grace, who rested upon thee in all his fullness:

the spirit of wisdom, enabling us to relish the fruit of the tree of life, which is indeed thyself;

the gift of understanding: to enlighten our perceptions;

the gift of prudence, enabling us to follow in thy footsteps;

the gift of strength: to withstand our adversary's onslaught;

the gift of knowledge: to distinguish good from evil by the light of thy holy teaching;

the gift of piety: to clothe ourselves with charity and mercy;

the gift of fear: to withdraw from all ill-doing and live quietly in awe of thy eternal majesty.

These are the things for which we petition. Grant them for the honor of thy holy name, to which, with the Father and the Holy Spirit, be all honor and glory, thanksgiving, renown, and lordship forever and ever. Amen.[53]

MUSEUM AND GROUNDS

The small museum contains the original mission doors, carved with wavy lines representing the "river of life," as well as books from the mission library, believed to be the second oldest library in California. In addition, there are intricate baskets of the Chumash and the mysterious wooden bells.

A Mexican tile fountain forms the focus of the mission gardens. The stone grotto is a shrine to Our Lady of the Apocalypse. Behind the mission and in front of Holy Cross School is a contemporary statue of the Native American St. Kateri Tekakwitha, a recognition of the Indians who built the mission.

"Queen of the Missions"

Founded on December 4, 1786

2201 Laguna Street

Santa Bárbara, CA 93105

www.santabarbaramission.org

This was the tenth of the California missions. St. Junípero Serra, the founder of the first nine, had planned to establish this mission, but he died before his vision could come to fruition. So the honor fell to Fr. Fermín Lasuén, Serra's successor as Father-President of the missions. He placed Fr. Paterna, a companion of Serra, in charge to put up the first buildings and make the first converts. The mission named for Santa Bárbara gradually earned its title, "Queen of the Missions," for its regal strength and graceful beauty.

Off the coast of Santa Bárbara lie the Channel Islands. Both the mainland and the islands were inhabited for thousands of years by the Chumash people. They were peaceful hunter-gatherers, living from the region's abundant natural resources and navigating the ocean with ease in *tomols*, artfully built sewn-plank canoes. Spanish maritime explorer Sebastián Vizcaíno gave the name Santa Bárbara to the channel and also one of the islands in gratitude for having survived a dense fog and storm while passing through the strait on the eve of her feast in 1602.

In 1782 a force of soldiers led by Governor Neve came to build a presidio in the area to protect California from foreign interests and to guard the missions from hostile attacks. Fr. Serra accompanied the expedition, and when a suitable site for the presidio was located, he blessed the land, planted the cross, and offered the Mass. Serra expected the governor to then authorize the establishment of a mission nearby, but he was informed that the mission would not be approved until the completion of the presidio. While Serra visited the presidio twice during the following year, he died a month before news arrived from a new governor that Mission Santa Bárbara could finally be established.

Fr. Lasuén chose a hilltop overlooking the presidio, the oaken valley, the blue sea, and the distant islands. The Indians called the place Tanayan (rocky mound). On December 4, 1786, Lasuén dedicated the mission to Santa Bárbara on the day of her feast. In the spring, the first buildings were erected with logs, and in time adobe buildings were constructed and the quadrangle completed.

For the Chumash neophytes, about 250 Indian houses were placed in rows to the left of the mission. They were plastered and whitewashed, with doors and movable windows. Near the mission was the village of Siutju, home to about five hundred Chumash who have been described in diaries as friendly, intelligent, and resourceful. Their leader, Chief Yanonali, became a Christian, leading many of the villagers to follow. About 4,700 of the natives were baptized over the years of the mission, and they worked at the various mission trades. The Indians made adobes, tiles, shoes, and woolen garments, learned the trades of carpenter and mason, and became herdsmen and farmers. They also learned to sing and play European instrumental music, and church services were accompanied by an Indian choir and instrumental ensemble of violins, cellos, woodwinds, and brasses.

The year before secularization, the Father-President Narciso Durán moved the headquarters for all the missions to Mission Santa Bárbara. In 1834, the Mexican government secularized the mission, ending its self-sufficiency and placing the Chumash under civil jurisdiction. But unlike the other missions, the Franciscans maintained control of Santa Bárbara. Fr. Durán was appointed administrator, and the first bishop of California, Francisco Garcia Diego y Moreno, OFM, also resided at the mission. Thus Santa Bárbara experienced less destruction during these years than the other missions. When both the bishop and Fr. Durán died in 1846, Governor Pio Pico attempted to confiscate the lands and sell the mission. He was, however, too late to effect much change, as this same year the occupation of California by the United States began.

When the mission period was over, the buildings were used for a number of purposes. A Franciscan missionary college functioned there from 1856 to 1885. A seminary operated there from 1886 to 1987. The Franciscan School of Theology resided there until 1968. The grounds are today used as a retreat center, and the mission church is used by the parish of Santa Bárbara.

When Fr. Durán moved the headquarters of the California missions here in 1833, he brought with him all the documents related to all the missions. Santa Bárbara then became the official repository for all the records of the California mission era. Among its treasures are the largest known collection of sheet music from the missions and other collections that have created this impressive compilation of documents. The archive library now occupies a portion of the mission building complex.

PATRON OF THE MISSION

Santa Bárbara (St. Barbara) was a fourth-century martyr. According to tradition, she was the daughter of the pagan Dioscorus, a wealthy man in the city of Heliopolis. Seeing that Bárbara was extraordinarily beautiful, her father shut her up in a tower until she should marry. By day she looked upon the hills, meadows, and rivers, and by night, the majestic, twinkling vault of the heavens. She desired to know the true God and Creator of all, and she decided to devote her life to this goal. When Bárbara refused all who sought her hand in marriage, her father permitted her to leave the seclusion of the tower. Bárbara met young Christian maidens in the city, and they taught her about the true faith. A priest baptized her, and she spent her life in virginity.

During this time, a luxurious bathhouse was being built at the house of Dioscorus. While he was away, Bárbara ordered the workers to create three windows to form a Trinity of light. On one of the walls of the bathhouse Bárbara etched a cross in the marble with her finger. Later, her footprints were imprinted on the stone steps of the bathhouse, and the water became an instrument for miraculous healings. When Dioscorus returned, he discovered his daughter's conversion and sought to have her killed. After being hidden for a while, she was arrested and tortured, and finally she was beheaded by her own father.

After Dioscorus carried out the deed, he was struck with a flash of lightening and died. The edifying legend of St. Bárbara became popular in the seventh century, and she became known as a protector against lightning, explosions, sudden death, and an unrepentant heart. St. Bárbara is often depicted in art next to a tower and wearing a crown of victory. In one hand she holds either a chalice or monstrance, as a sign that one devoted to her will not depart this life without the strength of the holy sacraments. In the other hand, she bears either a sword or a palm of martyrdom.

Mission Bells

The present church, dedicated in 1820, had only one bell tower. A second was added in 1833, making it the only California mission today with two towers. Each tower holds two tiers of bells, with six bells hanging within the towers today.

MISSION CHURCH

After the original church was ruined in the 1812 earthquake, the present stone church was begun. The outside façade is adapted from the design of an ancient Roman temple found by the padres in the mission library, and the capitals of the neoclassical columns are ionic style. Statues representing faith, hope, and charity stand on the three corners of the pediment, and in the center of the triangle rests a statue of St. Bárbara.

The interior of the church is lavishly painted in oranges, golds, blues, and greens, and the reredos behind the altar is a grand display of color and images. The eyes are drawn upward to the crucifix backed by a golden sunburst. Beneath is a richly colored statue of St. Bárbara. To the left is Mary the Immaculate Conception and to the right is St. Joseph. Below, to the left and right, are St. Francis and St. Dominic. A stone plaque embedded in the floor marks the crypt beneath the church where early missionaries are buried. Included are the founding missionary, Fr. Antonio Paterna, and Father-President Narciso Durán.

Two canvas paintings—eighteenth-century works that are the largest paintings in the missions—are situated at the transition from the nave to the sanctuary. One portrays the crucifixion of Christ, and the other depicts the Assumption and Coronation of Mary. Amidst the original Stations of the Cross that line the nave are two horizontal paintings. On one side is found the three archangels: Gabriel, Michael, and Raphael. On the opposite side are three Franciscan women: St. Agnes of Assisi, St. Clare of Assisi, and St. Margaret of Cortona.

At the rear of the church, the baptismal font stands beneath the choir loft. In side altars are remarkable sculptured scenes—each with its own painted arch and dome—which depict the Risen Jesus with Mary Magdalene and St. Francis and St. Clare of Assisi.

—PRAYER—

We adore You, Lord Jesus Christ, here, and in all your churches throughout the whole world, and we bless You, because by your holy Cross, You have redeemed the world (St. Francis of Assisi).

A READING FROM THE FIRST LETTER OF ST. PETER:

Blessed be the God and Father of our Lord Jesus Christ! By his great mercy he has given us a new birth into a living hope through the resurrection of Jesus Christ from the dead, and into an inheritance that is imperishable, undefiled, and unfading, kept in heaven for you, who are being protected by the power of God through faith for a salvation ready to be revealed in the last time. In this you rejoice, even if now for a little while you have had to suffer various trials, so that the genuineness of your faith—being more precious than gold that, though perishable, is tested by fire—may be found to result in praise and glory and honor when Jesus Christ is revealed. Although you have not seen him, you love him; and even though you do not see him now, you believe in him and rejoice with an indescribable and glorious joy, for you are receiving the outcome of your faith, the salvation of your souls (1 Peter 1:3–9).

V: From temptation, sin, and denial of our faith,

R: Deliver us, O Lord, in your mercy.

V: From fire, lightning, and earthquake,

R: Deliver us, O Lord, in your mercy.

V: From anxiety, danger, terror, and all evil,

R: Deliver us, O Lord, in your mercy.

V: From plague, famine, and war,

R: Deliver us, O Lord, in your mercy.

Let us pray:

Ever-living God, from whom faith draws perseverance and weakness draws strength, make us eager to receive the faith of your Church and courageous in confessing it. As we honor the victory of St. Bárbara, virgin and martyr, we pray, through her intercession, that we may bear every adversity for the sake of your love and lay down our lives in witness to Jesus our Lord. Amen.

MUSEUM AND GROUNDS

A side door of the church leads to the *camposanto*, the cemetery garden. The outside of the door contains three sets of skull and crossbones, used to designate a cemetery in Spanish colonial days. The cemetery dates from 1789, and over time around four thousand Native Americans were buried here, including Chumash chief Pedro Yanonali and numerous Spanish settlers. The opposite side of the church leads to the Sacred Garden, a meditation area that was once the mission quadrangle containing workshops for teaching trades to the natives, supply rooms, and residences. Today the garden features palm trees and roses, with a peaceful fountain in the center.

The museum is housed in the *convento*, originally the residence of the missionaries. One room is devoted to the culture of the Chumash, showcasing their plant-sewn canoes and fine basketwork. Another space shows the building process of the missions, presenting diagrams of the mission grounds. Another room features Chumash art, including the only surviving sculpture created by the Indians of California: images called Faith and Charity. The statue of Hope was lost or destroyed in an earthquake. The original statue of St. Bárbara is the finest piece in this display. These were brightly painted statues which, at one time, sat above the façade of the mission church. Replicas now take their place atop the church.

Other rooms display the mission trades taught to the natives, including candlemaking, pottery, weaving, ironwork, and the creation of paints for mission art. There are reconstructions of the *convento* rooms, including a typical missionary's bedroom, the *cocina* (kitchen) with its original adobe wall, and a room dedicated to Bishop Francisco Garcia Diego, the first bishop of California. The chapel room contains liturgical vestments, musical instruments, music scores, and sacred art. The mission's first tabernacle, made from polychrome wood and featuring abalone shell inlay and mirrored doors, was made around 1789 by local Indian artists.

To the right of the church, the outside wall of the cemetery leads to a portion of the original aqueduct, and across the street is the extension of the water channel in the park area. This aqueduct fed the mission with water, then flowed to the attractive fountain now in front of the mission and to the gardens and orchards. The water also flowed to the long pool in front of the fountain which served as the *lavadero* (laundry), with water spouts sculpted as the heads of mountain lions. At the base of the sloping lawn that spreads toward the ocean, there is a colorful garden of roses and cacti. The wooden cross at the base of the field is dedicated to St. Junípero Serra, pioneer missionary of California and founder of the town of Santa Bárbara.

OTHER NEARBY SIGHTS

Mission Historical Park. To the right of the mission grounds, this park preserves ruins of the mission's waterworks, built by Indian labor. It contains a filter house, grist mill, two reservoirs, and sections of aqueduct. Tannery vats, a pottery kiln, and the

City Rose Garden are found within the park. A dam, built in 1807, is located in the Santa Bárbara Botanic Garden, one and one-half miles up Mission Canyon.

The Presidio of Santa Bárbara. The presidio, established four years before the mission, is located in the heart of downtown Santa Bárbara. It served as military headquarters and governmental center for the Spanish in the coastal region. The original presidio consisted of residences, a chapel, guardhouses, storerooms, and armories built in a square around the *plaza de armas* (parade grounds). The presidio chapel today is an accurate reconstruction of the mission-era church. Santa Bárbara occupies the top niche above the altar. Below her are St. Francis, the Madonna and Child, and St. Anthony of Padua. Paintings on either side of the sanctuary depict Christ the Good Shepherd and Our Lady of Solitude. The chapel was the primary place of worship for the residents as the pueblo or town of Santa Bárbara developed around the presidio.

On the back side of the chapel is the reconstructed *comandancia* (living quarters of the presidio's *comandante*). Built in 1787, it consisted of an entrance hall, living room, office, and bedroom. Buildings on the other side of Santa Bárbara Street display a mural depicting the presidio and the mission, a list of supplies needed by the presidio, living quarters for the families of soldiers, and native plants from the medicinal lore of the Chumash. Across Canon Perdido Street stands the oldest building in Santa Bárbara, El Cuartel. This small adobe served as the guardhouse and was part of a row of soldiers' quarters.

Channel Islands National Park. Across the Santa Bárbara Channel are the islands where many of the Chumash lived for thousands of years. Five of these islands today compose Channel Islands National Park, preserving a wealth of natural

and cultural resources. These may be visited by boat from Santa
Bárbara. Recreational activities on the islands include hiking,
camping, snorkeling, kayaking, birdwatching, or just relaxing to
the soothing sounds of the natural world. The easiest to access is
Santa Cruz Island, named for a Franciscan staff accidentally left
on the island during the Portolá expedition of 1769. According
to the story, a Chumash Indian found the cross-tipped staff and
returned it to the priest. The Spaniards were so impressed that
they called this island of friendly people La Isla de Santa Cruz
(Island of the Holy Cross).

"Mission of the Passes"
Founded on September 17, 1804
1760 Mission Drive
Solvang, CA 93463
www.missionsantaines.org

The mission was founded by Fr. Estevan Tápis and named in honor of St. Agnes, a Christian martyr of the fourth century. This was the nineteenth mission and the last mission founded in southern California. The native name for the site was Alajulapu, and it was situated in the land of the Chumash people, with many rancherías in the area. Overlooking a fertile valley and surrounding mountains, it has been designated the "Mission of the Passes," located near the mountain passes that connect the valley and the ocean to the south.

The mission site was chosen as a midway point between Mission Santa Bárbara and Mission La Purísima Concepción, and it was designed both to relieve overcrowding at those two missions and to serve the Indians living beyond the coastal mountain range. At the founding Mass—attended by two hundred Chumash—twenty-seven children were baptized and fifteen men came forward for instructions. By the end of the year, there were 112 neophytes, as the mission continued to grow rapidly and prosper.

As with many other missions, disaster struck with the earthquake of 1812, which destroyed most of the church and many of the adobe buildings of the quadrangle. Reconstruction began soon thereafter, and the new church was dedicated in 1817. The new walls were five feet thick, with heavy pine timbers from the mountains supporting the roof. Fr. Francisco Javier Uría is credited with both the design of the church and the elaborate water system, which was built to bring water from the mountains to serve the needs of the mission and the Indian village.

Mexico's independence from Spain brought heightened tension between the Indians and the Spanish soldiers. Because the soldiers were no longer being paid a salary from the government, they forced the Indians to work harder, longer, and without compensation, which fueled dissension. The pent-up unrest of the Indians turned into revolt in 1824 when a Spanish guard at the mission flogged an Indian neophyte. The Chumash attacked the mission, holding both priests and soldiers hostage and burning barracks and workshops. When the church caught fire, however, the Indians immediately helped extinguish it, stating that their quarrel was with the military and not the padres. The Indians fled to Mission La Purísima and took over the mission grounds for about a month until soldiers from Monterey quelled the revolt.

When the mission was secularized, the Franciscans were able to keep the church and their lodgings. In 1844, Governor Micheltorena donated acreage adjacent to the mission for California's first seminary, the College of Our Lady Refuge of Sinners. In the seminary's constitution, there is a provision for the education of the sons of the local ranchers, whose tuition helped maintain the college.

Although the mission was never totally abandoned, the buildings fell into disrepair. Maintenance was so neglected that one Sunday in the 1860s the high pulpit collapsed while the flabbergasted padre was preaching. It seems that it was never replaced. In 1904, the centennial of the mission's founding, Fr. Alexander Buckler, with the aid of his niece Mamie Goulet, began a twenty-year restoration of the mission. The Capuchin Franciscan priests arrived in 1924 and undertook more extensive renovation, a work that continues today.

PATRON OF THE MISSION

Santa Inés (St. Agnes) was a Roman maiden of about thirteen years of age who was martyred during the persecutions of Emperor Diocletian in 304. Early Christian poets and writers extol her virginity and heroism under torture for her faith. When she rejected her many young suitors, they submitted her to the authorities as a Christian believer. Then, refusing to worship pagan idols, she was put into a fire but remained unharmed by the flames. When she was finally beheaded, her body was placed in a catacomb on the Via Nomentana outside of Rome.

During the time of Constantine, the first Christian emperor, a basilica was built over her tomb. This was replaced in the seventh century by the structure now standing. Every year, on the feast of St. Agnes, January 21, two lambs are blessed by the pope. Their wool is then woven into pallia, the ceremonial neck-stoles given by the pope to the newly elevated archbishops throughout the world to symbolize their union with the papacy.

St. Agnes is one of seven women commemorated by name in the Roman Canon. Her name is derived from the Greek word meaning "pure," but because it sounds like the Latin word *agnus* (lamb), the lamb became her symbol and she is often depicted in art holding a lamb. In a painting in the mission museum, she is depicted holding the lily for purity and the palm for triumph in martyrdom.

MISSION BELLS

An adobe bell wall was erected for two bells and dedicated in 1817 with new bells cast in Lima, Peru. The bell wall lasted until 1911 when a huge rainstorm literally melted it. When

Fr. Buckler had it rebuilt the following year out of reinforced concrete, a third bell arch was added.

Today, the mission museum displays four bells. The 1804 bell, named for Juan Baptista, is the oldest. The Ave Maria Purísima bell was cast in 1807, and the bell from Lima was cast in 1817. Still hanging in the top arch of the bell wall is the second bell from Lima, which was recast in 1953. A bell named for St. Agnes, dated 1881, was used for the dedication of the new tower in 1912. Finally, two new bells were dedicated in 1984, named for St. Agnes and St. Francis.

MISSION CHURCH

The church looks very much like it looked to its Chumash worshipers in 1817. A statue of Santa Inés, the patron of the mission, crowns the area of the altar in a central niche and is thought to be created by native artists. Below the crucifix is a tabernacle with a lovely painted door of the Good Shepherd. This small painting portrays Christ as a young man with a sheep over his shoulders. He is dressed in a bluish cloak and wears a straw hat with upturned brim. The image is painted with oils on wood and surrounded by an elaborate frame characteristic of the Mexican baroque.

The decorations throughout the church were created under the direction of skilled artisans with access to pattern books of neoclassical design. Designs outside the altar rail appear to have been done by neophyte artists. The nave and ceiling were painted in vegetable colors by Indians. The floor tiles and all but two of the ceiling beams are original.

Statues and paintings from the mission years are found throughout the church. On a side altar, the statue of Our Lady of the Rosary, a Mexican baroque sculpture from the mid-eighteenth century, is particularly beautiful. The fourteen Stations of the Cross are oil on canvas from late eighteenth-century Mexico. Inside the baptistery, beneath a statue of St. John the Baptist, is a font of zinc and copper made by the mission neophytes.

—PRAYER—

We adore You, Lord Jesus Christ, here, and in all your churches throughout the whole world, and we bless You, because by your holy Cross, You have redeemed the world (St. Francis of Assisi).

A READING FROM THE GOSPEL ACCORDING TO ST. MATTHEW:
"The kingdom of heaven is like treasure hidden in a field, which someone found and hid; then in his joy he goes and sells all that he has and buys that field. Again, the kingdom of heaven is like a merchant in search of fine pearls; on finding one pearl of great value, he went and sold all that he had and bought it" (Matthew 13:44–46).

V: "Christ is my Spouse," said St. Agnes. "He chose me first and I'll be his."

R: St. Agnes, virgin and martyr, pray for us.

V: "He made my soul beautiful with the jewels of grace and virtue. I belong to Him Whom angels serve."

R: St. Agnes, virgin and martyr, pray for us.

V: "Holy Father, hear me. I am coming to you whom I have loved, whom I have sought and always desired."

R: St. Agnes, virgin and martyr, pray for us.

V: Unfailing model of perseverance, invincible champion of chastity, shining mirror of virtue.

R: St. Agnes, virgin and martyr, pray for us.

Let us pray:

Ever-living God, who chooses those who are weak to confound the strong, look with mercy on all young people whose goodness is threatened by the snares of the world. Help them find inspiring guides and true friends to accompany them in following the Lamb of God and finding safe pastures in his Church. Through the intercession of Felicity, Perpetua, Agatha, Lucy, Agnes, Cecilia, Anastasia, and all holy martyrs, lead us all to persevere until death and gain the crown of eternal life.

MUSEUM AND GROUNDS

Mission Santa Inés has a rich collection of paintings and statuary. The painting of St. Agnes in the Mission Museum was done by Andres Lopez in Mexico City in 1803. The portrait of the archangel Raphael was painted by a Chumash neophyte. The liturgical vestments are a valuable collection from the fifteenth century to 1718, including a chasuble reputedly worn by St. Junipero Serra. The vestments are made of materials such as oriental silks, with floral designs, satins, damasks, and brocades, transformed into Spanish and Roman style chasubles. There are also Bibles, missals, and music manuscripts for the mission choir and orchestra. The beautifully produced manuscripts are primarily plainsong, which is one-line, homophonic music sung to Latin texts.

The last of the museum rooms is dedicated to the Madonna. A statue of Our Lady of Sorrows gazes upward toward a crucifix. Other images of the Holy Mother occupy the small room. A tile on the floor, the one with the painted square, holds the footprint of a Chumash, one of those whose hard work made the bricks and built the mission.

A fountain forms the center of the mission garden. Palm and olive trees, roses, and cacti, along with several outdoor shrines create a meditative area. In the back part, a portion of the asphalt floor of the former seminary has been uncovered. Also toward the rear is described the story of Pasquala, an Indian girl who ran from her village to warn Fr. Uria of the rebellion of 1824. The *camposanto* (cemetery) stretches on the opposite side of the church, with various crosses and headstones representing the 1,700 neophytes, soldiers, priests, and settlers buried here.

OTHER NEARBY SIGHTS

Solvang. The Danish town of Solvang was built up around the mission in the early 1900s. The quaint village offers shops with Danish cuisine and pastries.

MISSION LA PURÍSIMA CONCEPCIÓN

"Linear Mission"
Founded on December 8, 1787
2295 Purísima Road
Lompoc, CA 93436
www.lapurisimamission.org

Father-President Fermín Lasuén founded this mission to honor "The Immaculate Conception of Mary Most Holy" on her feast in 1787. The mission is the last of the three missions planned for the Santa Bárbara Channel, thus closing the gap between the missions of the northern and southern clusters. The mission is sometimes called the "Linear Mission" because it is the only mission to be built in a linear shape rather than as a quadrangle. Today the mission is a living history museum maintained by California State Parks. It is the most thoroughly reconstructed of all the missions and provides the best setting for understanding what mission life was like.

The original mission was established four miles from the present site, in what is now downtown Lompoc. It was productive from the beginning, with fertile land and a population of eager Chumash converts. By the turn of the century, the mission had outgrown its first church, so a new church was constructed and finished in 1802. By 1812, under the leadership of Fr. Mariano Payéras, the mission produced abundant crops and maintained a growing herd of more than twenty thousand livestock. But after flourishing for twenty-five years, the earthquake of December 1812 struck for four minutes, badly damaging the walls of the church. Then, a half hour later, the second quake shattered most of the buildings. The winter rains, floods, and mudslides damaged the mission beyond repair.

Lesser men than Fr. Payéras and the frontier missionaries would have accepted defeat, but the mission enterprise had more than a thousand homeless neophytes to shelter, feed, and clothe. The Franciscans selected a new site, in the "valley of the watercress," upon which to rebuild the mission. This new site had several advantages: a better water supply, a better climate, and a closer access to El Camino Real, California's main travel route. After erecting temporary shelters, work began on new and finer construction, and within a few years, the mission once again became a thriving community. The many shops for mission enterprises became a training center for the inhabitants, producing soap, candles, wool, and leather products among their leading commodities.

The unique foresight, dedication, and organizational skills of Fr. Payéras did not go unnoticed, and he was appointed Father-President of the California missions in 1815. Rather than forsake La Purísima, he made it the headquarters for all the missions. In 1823, his body finally gave way to the rigors of mission life. He is buried under the altar of the mission church.

With the loss of the exceptional guidance of Fr. Payéras, the mission began to decline. When Mexico gained independence from Spain, the missions no longer received supplies and the soldiers received no pay. They vented their frustrations with increasingly cruel acts toward the Indians, until the inevitable revolt of the natives came in 1824 throughout the three missions of the Santa Bárbara Channel. Although the Indians seized the mission and held it for nearly a month, the soldiers from Monterey lifted the siege in three hours, leaving sixteen Indians dead and many wounded. As a result, the governor and military condemned seven Indians to death and sentenced eighteen others to imprisonment and hard labor.

Once mission assets were civilly administered after secularization, landholdings were divided up, the neophytes were released
from any supervision, and a *mayordomo* (administrator) was
appointed over the mission by the governor. The neophytes
were no longer free to engage in activities beneficial to themselves, but were required to fill government orders for grains,
blankets, saddles, shoes, and the needs of the soldiers and their
families. The mission lands were gradually sold and given away
by the government and the Indians scattered. In 1845, Governor
Pico sold the mission, with all its lands and treasures, to Juan
Temple of Los Angeles for $1,110. It subsequently changed
hands and uses a number of times prior to the close of the nineteenth century.

The crumbling ruins were rescued in the 1930s by the Civilian
Conservation Corps and the National Parks Service. The
mission site became a public works project, under the direction of a staff of archeologists, historians, architects, and engi-
neers. The entire mission was rebuilt, using mission-era tools
and methods whenever possible. When complete, the mission
was considered one of the finest historical reconstructions of its
day and a national treasure. In 1973, a volunteer organization
was formed called *Prelado de los Tesoros de la Purísima* (The
Keepers of the Treasures of La Purísima). Their goal is bringing
the mission to life so that visitors gain a firsthand understanding
and appreciation of California's history.

PATRON OF THE MISSION

La Purísima Concepción de María Santísima (The Immaculate
Conception of Mary Most Holy) is a title of Mary, celebrated
annually on December 8, the founding date of the mission. The
title expresses the traditional belief that Mary, because she was
chosen by God to be mother of the Redeemer, was filled with

grace from the moment of her own conception and remained always free from sin. Although the dogma was only officially declared by Pope Pius IX in 1854, the doctrine had strong support through the centuries, especially in Spain and among the Franciscans. La Purísima Mission was the first of two California missions dedicated to Mary, the Mother of the Lord.

The iconography of the Immaculate Conception shows Mary standing with her hands in prayer, derived from the traditional art of her Assumption. The crescent moon below her feet and other imagery comes from the book of Revelation: "A great portent appeared in heaven: a woman clothed with the sun, with the moon under her feet, and on her head a crown of twelve stars" (Revelation 12:1). Many Spanish and Mexican artists produced representations of the Immaculate Conception. The image of Our Lady of Guadalupe—found in statues and paintings in many of the missions—is one of the earliest examples of this type.

MISSION BELLS

In the absence of drawings or descriptions of the original campanario, the reconstruction was copied on the one at neighboring Mission Santa Inés. The pinkish color matches the original plaster. The tower has two rolling bells in the lower tier and one stationary bell above. Cast in Lima, Peru, the bronze bells were skillfully tuned and balanced to produce together a wide range of tones. Seen from the cemetery, the back side of the tower reveals the reconstructed stairway and the platform for the bell ringer.

MISSION CHURCH

The church has been nicely rebuilt and refurnished. Located in a state historic park, it is not an active church today, but is still a sacred space for remembrance and prayer. The walls are painted in shades of pink, blue, gold, and green, with geometric and floral designs. Abalone shells are placed in wall niches for

 holding holy water, and a baptismal font rests on a pedestal by the rear doorway. Oil paintings and Stations of the Cross line the walls, while a polychrome statue of the young Jesus with hands upraised is preserved behind glass opposite the front doorway.

The tabernacle rests on the altar. It is inlaid with abalone shells and ornamented with elements of the passion of Christ. In niches above rest statues of the saints: the Madonna in the center, with St. Joseph and St. Anthony of Padua on each side holding the Christ child. On the floor of the sanctuary is a grave marker for Fr. Payéras, born in Mallorca, Spain, in 1769, and died here in 1823, after spending nineteen years in service to this mission.

The tiles in the rear of the church are original. Without benches or pews as in today's churches, the neophytes stood, sat, or kneeled on this bare tiled floor. The men and boys of the mission choir sang from here, while the musicians played in the loft above.

—Prayer—

We adore You, Lord Jesus Christ, here, and in all your churches throughout the whole world, and we bless You, because by your holy Cross, You have redeemed the world (St. Francis of Assisi).

A READING FROM THE BOOK OF REVELATION:

A great portent appeared in heaven: a woman clothed with the sun, with the moon under her feet, and on her head a crown of twelve stars. She was pregnant and was crying out in birthpangs, in the agony of giving birth. Then another portent appeared in heaven: a great red dragon, with seven heads and ten horns, and seven diadems on his heads. His tail swept down a third of the stars of heaven and threw them to the earth. Then the dragon stood before the woman who was about to bear a child, so that he might devour her child as soon as it was born. And she gave birth to a son, a male child, who is to rule all the nations with a rod of iron. But her child was snatched away and taken to God and to his throne; and the woman fled into the wilderness, where she has a place prepared by God (Revelation 12:1–6).

Salutation to Mary, the Mother of God, by St. Francis of Assisi:

Hail, O Lady, Holy Queen, Mary, holy Mother of God,

You are Virgin made Church, chosen by the most Holy Father in heaven whom He consecrated with His most holy and beloved Son and with the Holy Spirit the Paraclete, in whom there was and is all fullness of grace and every good.

Hail His Palace! Hail His Tabernacle! Hail His Dwelling!

Hail His Robe! Hail His Servant! Hail His Mother!

And hail all you holy virtues which are poured into the hearts of the faithful through the grace and enlightenment of the Holy Spirit, that from being unbelievers, you may make them faithful to God. Amen.[54]

Let us pray:

O God, who endowed the Blessed Virgin Mary with the rich fullness of your grace and preserved her from all sin, may she be for us a model of holiness and a perfect image of your Church. Grant that, through her intercession, we may be freed from sin and enter into your presence forever. Amen.

MUSEUM AND GROUNDS

A tour of the mission either begins or ends in the Visitor Center and Exhibit Hall, the modern building above the parking lot. The exhibits showcase artifacts and descriptions of Chumash culture and the history of the mission from its founding to the present.

Crossing over the footbridge brings the visitor into the mission as it looked in the early nineteenth century. The mission stood on the Camino Real, so travelers could stop here on their journey between missions to share news of the world. The mission raised longhorn cattle, Churro sheep, horses, donkeys, goats, pigs, turkeys, and chickens, some of which are represented in the livestock pens.

To the right of the bell tower and church, the *cuartel*, or soldiers' barracks, displays cots, weapons, and other equipment. The corporal's quarters lead to the interior courtyard, with its oven for baking bread, fire pits for cooking stew, and tables for eating. Another apartment housed the *mayordomo*, the Spanish or Indian foreman responsible for managing the crops and herds. In this courtyard, the burro was employed to turn the stone for grinding olives, then the crushed olives were squeezed in the press to produce the oil. The shops in this area include a room for making candles from tallow, the carpentry shop, and the weaving room, where women and children were taught to spin wool and weave blankets and shawls.

The next building is the Franciscan residence. The colonnade along the front features uniquely designed pillars, half of which are original and half reconstructed. Along the corridor are rooms where the padres lived, prayed, and directed the work of the mission. The second church at the mission was originally the chapel of the padres, but it was remodeled when the main church was destroyed by an underground spring. The chapel is simple in design and features the Immaculate Conception in its central niche. The next room is the large *sala* (living room), where the padres entertained guests and negotiated trade. Other rooms include bedrooms and a guestroom, followed by the mission office, which kept the mission records and the library.

Behind the residence, the pottery shop produced thousands of tiles for floors and roofs, clay pipes for the water system, and dishes, all of which were fired in the kiln outside. In the community kitchen, the Indian women prepared meals for the mission inhabitants. In the grist mill, a burro would turn the wheel to grind wheat and barley into flour for cooking. The blacksmith shop contains the original forge, where metal is heated for shaping on the anvil with hammer, chisel, fuller, and hardy.

A footbridge and path leads to the springhouse. Water from nearby springs was collected here, filtered through sand, and channeled underground through clay pipes to the mission. Nearer the mission, the fountain, cistern, and lavanderia for washing form parts of the water system. The mission gardens contain mission-era plants that were used for food, fiber, medicine, and perfume for the mission's apartments.

Nearby, various Indian dwellings may be seen. Homes built of tule reed represent the traditional dwellings of the Chumash. Other Indians dwelt in adobe apartments. The *monjerio* is the girl's dormitory, where girls between age eleven and marriage lived and learned to cook, sew, and weave. They visited their families by day but had to be back in the dormitory at night. The mission infirmary cared for the many illnesses caused by exposure to European diseases.

The mission website offers a program guide that provides dates for special events. The volunteers of the Prelado, the keepers of the treasures, provide high-quality and unique programs, candlelight tours, and Founding Day celebrations with Mass and concert on December 8.

OTHER NEARBY SIGHTS

Mission Vieja. Mission Vieja in Lompoc is the site of the original mission before the earthquake of 1812 destroyed it. There is little left of this mission, but its remnants may be explored by following the interpretive paths.

"Prince of the Missions"

Founded on September 1, 1772

751 Palm Street

San Luis Obispo CA 93401

www.missionsanluisobispo.org

This fifth of the California missions was founded by St. Junípero Serra on September 1, 1772. Serra decided that the area's natural resources and friendly Chumash people made it an ideal site for the next mission. With soldiers, muleteers, and pack animals carrying mission supplies, he set out for the place. Raising the cross near a creek described as having "the finest water," Serra offered the founding Mass but then left the responsibility of the mission's construction to Fr. José Cavaller. This mission is sometimes designated as the "Prince of the Missions," or the "Mission in the Valley of Bears."

While exploring the valley in 1769, the expedition of Gaspar de Portolá came upon an area that was full of holes and torn-up soil. They soon discovered that the area had an abundance of bears, all of them looking for their favorite roots to eat. Thereafter called by the Spaniards *La Cañada de los Osos* (The Valley of the Bears), Fr. Serra remembered the place in 1772 when rations were dwindling and the first four missions were facing starvation. He sent a hunting expedition to kill grizzlies and send back the meat to the missions. After great success, the men loaded the pack mules with nine thousand pounds of salted and jerked bear meat for the missions. In addition, they sent back twenty-five loads of edible seeds that they had received from the Indians in exchange for meat. The natives were impressed at the ease by which the Spanish could take down the huge grizzlies with their firearms.

But as this fifth mission began, supplies were again at a minimum. The missionaries came with only five soldiers and two neophytes, but the men survived with the help of the genial Chumash, who supplemented their meager food supplies and shortly began helping them build the mission structures. Soon many were persuaded to bring their children to be baptized, and a settlement of neophytes grew up around the mission.

Not all of the Indians were as cordial to the Spaniards as the neophytes, however, and hostile tribes to the east beleaguered the mission in its early years. In 1776, an arrow with a burning wick attached was shot into one of the dry, thatched roofs of the mission, starting a fire that destroyed all the buildings except the church and granary. When similar attacks followed over the years, the missionaries were forced to develop more secure structures. In 1790, the mission began to manufacture its own roof tiles—a great advance over thatch for roofing because they resisted both fire and rain.

In time, the mission quadrangle included a *convento*, warehouses, workshops, and residences. Many of the most prosperous years were overseen by Fr. Luis Antonio Martinez, remembered as a generous, humorous, and effective priest who served the mission for more than thirty years. Martinez also had a quick temper and was an outspoken critic of the governor. Eventually he was arrested on a flimsy charge, accused of treason, and deported in 1830, much to the disappointment of the Indians.

As Fr. Martinez had foreseen, the mission was secularized five years after his banishment. Within a few years, the value of the mission property dwindled to almost nothing, and it was sold at a public auction for a few hundred dollars. Like several other missions, San Luis Obispo soon became the nucleus of a flourishing town. In the last half of the nineteenth century, the mission property was used not only as a parish church, but also as the town's schoolhouse, jail, and courthouse.

Restoration began in the 1930s. Today the mission functions as a parish church and is the center of the busy downtown area. Mission Plaza stands in front of the church, with its fountain depicting statues of a Chumash child and a family of bears.

PATRON OF THE MISSION

San Luis Obispo de Tolosa (St. Louis Bishop of Toulouse) was born a prince in southern France in 1274. He was the second son of King Charles of Naples and Mary, the daughter of King Stephen V of Hungary. Through his parents, he was the great nephew of two holy figures: St. Louis, King of France and St. Elisabeth of Hungary.

After France was defeated in battle with Spain, Louis and his brother were sent, as hostages, to Spain for the release of their father. The brothers spent seven years in Spain, being instructed by Franciscan friars. After absorbing their teaching, Louis decided to join the order. Upon his release, he renounced his claim to the crown of Naples in favor of his brother and made his religious profession as a Franciscan friar in Rome.

Bowing to the will of Pope Boniface VIII, he was consecrated the next year as Bishop of Toulouse. He traveled to his diocese as a poor religious, but was received at Toulouse with the splendor befitting a prince and the devotion befitting a saint. His first concern was providing for the relief of the indigent, and his first visits were made to the hospitals and the poor. In his service to his diocese, he inspired many with his preaching, austerity, and dedication.

He did not, however, live to serve his diocese, for he fell ill while traveling to Provence and died of a fever on August 19, 1297, at the young age of twenty-three. Renowned for his sanctity, he was canonized a few years later in 1317. His relics rest today in the cathedral at Valencia in Spain.

Images of San Luis Obispo depict him as a young man, wearing splendid episcopal vestments over a simple Franciscan habit. He wears a bishop's mitre, holds a crozier, and is sometimes shown with his forsaken royal crown at his feet.

MISSION BELLS

Five new bells—named after the patrons of the first five missions—were dedicated for the mission tower in 2005. As seen from the plaza, they are, from left to right, Carlos, Diego, Antonio, Gabriel, and Luis. The older bells are now displayed on the grounds.

The job of mission bell ringer, usually the assignment of an Indian, required serious training. A whole vocabulary of bell patterns had to be learned because the bells were a communication mechanism for the whole community. The most famous bell ringers at the mission were Florentino Naja and Gregorio Silverio. In 1820, when bells were installed from Lima, Peru, a teenaged Chumash Indian, Florentino Naja, was instructed by the padres in the art of bell ringing. He rang the bells for seventy-four years, until his death in 1894, and in the last two years of his life, he taught his young apprentice, Gregorio Silverio. When Naja died, Silverio took over the bell-ringing at the age of thirteen and held the position for sixty years, until his death in 1954.

MISSION CHURCH

Overlooking Mission Plaza, the façade of the church is unadorned. Archways lead into the porch area in front of the church doors, and matching arches above house the five bells. This combination of belfry and vestibule is unique among the missions of California.

Inside the church, the nave is long and narrow. The Stations of the Cross line the walls, lit by small windows above. The sanctuary is composed of small columns and simulated marble, framing the central image of Christ on the cross. To the left and right of the cross are statues of Mary the Immaculate Conception and St. Joseph with the child Jesus.

On the left side of the sanctuary stands a statue of St. Louis, Bishop of Toulouse. The statue is carved from wood, coated with gesso, gilded with gold leaf, painted, and fitted with glass eyes. During restoration, two layers of prior refurbishment had to be removed to find the original. This statue of the mission's patron faces the annex, added to the right of the sanctuary. Niches and shelves along the walls hold statues, paintings, the Blessed Sacrament altar, and a prayer room. The door of the annex opens out to the gardens alongside the church.

—PRAYER—

We adore You, Lord Jesus Christ, here, and in all your churches throughout the whole world, and we bless You, because by your holy Cross, You have redeemed the world (St. Francis of Assisi).

A READING FROM THE BOOK OF THE PROPHET EZEKIEL:

For thus says the Lord GOD: I myself will search for my sheep, and will seek them out. As shepherds seek out their flocks when they are among their scattered sheep, so I will seek out my sheep. I will rescue them from all the places to which they have been scattered on a day of clouds and thick darkness. I will bring them out from the peoples and gather them from the countries, and will bring them into their own land; and I will feed them on the mountains of Israel, by the watercourses, and in all the inhabited parts of the land. I will feed them with good pasture, and the mountain heights of Israel shall be their pasture; there they shall lie down in good grazing land, and they shall feed on rich pasture on the mountains of Israel. I myself will be the shepherd of my sheep, and I will make them lie down, says the Lord GOD. I will seek the lost, and I will bring back the strayed, and I will bind up the injured, and I will strengthen the weak, but the fat and the strong I will destroy. I will feed them with justice (Ezekiel 34:11–16).

V: We pray for bishops, pastors, presidents, governors, and all leaders of church and state, that they may guide their people like the good shepherd guides the flock.

R: The good shepherd lays down his life for the sheep (John 10:11).

V: For royalty, nobility, elected leaders, and all who rule over others, that they may have the gifts of wisdom and humility.

R: The good shepherd lays down his life for the sheep.

V: For spouses, that they may honor one another, for parents and children, that they may cherish one another, and for members of communities, that they may serve one another.

R: The good shepherd lays down his life for the sheep.

V: For all missionary disciples, that we may seek the lost, bring back the strayed, bind up the injured, and strengthen the weak.

R: The good shepherd lays down his life for the sheep.

Let us pray:

Lord God, who has appointed leaders to guide your people, watch over those chosen to show us the way. Through the intercession of San Luis Obispo, inspire wise and humble shepherds to serve their flocks. Give each of us the grace to care for those entrusted to us and to direct them in the ways of your kingdom. We pray this in the name of Jesus the Good Shepherd. Amen.

MUSEUM AND GROUNDS

The museum and gift shop is displayed in the mission *convento*. The first rooms feature paintings on the walls representing Chumash art and various aspects of native life. Tule reeds used to build the original roofs for the mission are displayed with some painted roof tiles that replaced the reeds and protected the mission from fire and rain. Basketry, shell and stone beads and necklaces, flintknapped points, stone tools, and other artifacts show how the natives lived both before and during missionary times.

Other rooms display religious artifacts from the mission. The tabernacle, crucifix, bells, clapper (used instead of the bells during Lent), and liturgical vestments all date to the mission era. A final room features items from more recent history, showing how a dining room would have looked in the early twentieth century.

OTHER NEARBY SIGHTS

San Luis Obispo town and creek. San Luis Obispo is a university town and a tourist mecca, filled with boutiques, restaurants, and coffee houses. Throughout much of the town, walking paths run alongside San Luis Obispo Creek. This waterway, so important to the Chumash and the mission, has been transformed today into a recreation area. Walk out of the mission to Mission Plaza to find a path down to the creek.

"Mission on the Highway"
Founded on July 25, 1797
775 Mission Street
San Miguel, CA 93451
www.missionsanmiguel.org

This sixteenth of the California missions was established by Fr. Fermín Lasuén, the third of four missions that he founded during the summer of 1797. Built right alongside El Camino Real and designated the "Mission on the Highway," it filled a long gap in the chain between the missions of San Antonio de Padua and San Luis Obispo. Fr. Buenaventura Sitjar, who was sent by Fr. Lasuén to find the site for the mission, was appointed administrator. He was fluent in the local Salinan language and had already ministered for almost twenty-five years at the nearby Mission San Antonio. The site he chose was called "Vahiá" or "Vahca" by the native population. The land was level and ideal for growing wheat, and there was abundant water from the San Miguel River and several springs in the area.

On the founding day, July 25, 1797, a large congregation was present for the Mass, and fifteen Indian children were baptized. Some Indian families from these two adjacent missions came to live near the new settlement and help with the construction, and they won the confidence of the other natives with their enthusiasm for mission life. A church was quickly built, along with a small village, thanks to the willing and hard-working natives. Over the next four years, there were more than a thousand converts from among the Salinan people.

The first chapel on the site was replaced within a year of its construction by a larger adobe chapel to accommodate the growing population of neophytes. But this chapel and the surrounding buildings filled with leather hides, wool, cloth, and wheat, were burned in a devastating fire in 1806. The church that stands today was built between 1816 and 1818. Because the neophytes had made tens of thousands of adobe bricks and clay roof tiles, the large church was built in an amazingly short time

Shortly after its founding, Fr. Juan Martin arrived at San Miguel. A jovial and generous Franciscan, he would lead the building efforts and effectively shepherd the mission for nearly twenty-seven years until his death in 1824. In 1820, he recruited Estevan Munras, a native of Barcelona, Spain, to decorate the interior of the church. Assisted by native artists, Munras created the colorful frescoes, using stencils and local pigments moistened with cactus juice. San Miguel is the only mission church in California to retain its original wall paintings.

After the last Franciscan left in 1841, the Salinan Indians dispersed, and the buildings were sold, with portions rented for a store, warehouse, dance hall, and saloon. The property was returned to the Church by order of President Buchanan in 1859, and the mission was reactivated as a parish in 1878. Badly damaged in the earthquake of 2003, the mission has since been repaired and preserved.

PATRON OF THE MISSION

San Miguel Arcángel (St. Michael the Archangel) is one of three archangels mentioned in the Bible. He is celebrated in the Jewish, Christian, and Islamic traditions. His Hebrew name means "Who is like God." In the book of Daniel, Michael is described as "the great prince," the protector of God's people (Daniel 12:1). In the New Testament letter of Jude, he is called "the archangel Michael" who contended with the devil (Jude 9). The book of Revelation describes Michael as God's great warrior who leads God's armies against the dragon, the forces of Satan (Revelation 12:7).

In Christian tradition, St. Michael the Archangel is invoked as the guardian and protector of the Church. He is the patron of all those who are in danger, particularly members of the armed forces, police officers, and firefighters. He is usually depicted as winged warrior, subduing a dragon or figure of Satan with a sword. He sometimes is shown carrying a set of scales for the weighing of souls at their death. Paintings and statues of the archangel are found throughout the California missions. The feast of the archangels Michael, Gabriel, and Raphael, is celebrated on September 29.

MISSION BELLS

During the mission era, San Miguel Arcángel never had a bell tower, but bells were hung from a wooden beam in the archways of the mission. The bell that hangs there today was cast in Mexico City in 1800. Today a belfry, containing a large bell and two small bells, stands toward the back of the mission property. The main, two thousand–pound bell was recast in 1888 from six cracked and broken bells in San Francisco.

MISSION CHURCH

The extraordinary frescoes within the church were painted by Salinan artists under the direction of Spanish artist Estevan Munras. The colors, made with local pigments, remain vivid. The central statue is a colorful image of St. Michael the Archangel, holding the scales of justice in his hand. To his left is a statue of St. Francis of Assisi, with one foot on a skull to indicate Christ's conquest of death, and to the right is St. Anthony of Padua, originally holding the infant Christ.

High above St. Michael is the all-seeing "Eye of God," shown in clouds surrounded by divine rays, a reminder of the watchful and caring presence of God. The columns on each side of the statues are painted to look like alabaster marble. They have fluted bases and Egyptian-like capitals. Above the image of St. Francis is the Franciscan coat of arms, showing the bare arm of Christ and the sleeved arm of Francis—both with the stigmata in their hands. Above the image of St. Anthony is another Franciscan coat of arms representing the five wounds received by Christ and St. Francis.

In the sanctuary to the left is an image of the Blessed Mother within a drawing of a columned temple. On the opposite side is St. Joseph within a duplicate fresco of a temple. Surrounding these two temples, the walls are drawn to resemble hanging pieces of embroidered silk. Further along the nave, on each side, are frescoes of large shells. These abalone shells were treasured by the Salinan people and were used by the padres in baptisms. Two Franciscans are buried near the Blessed Mother altar: Fr. Marcelino Cipres and Fr. Juan Martin. These two came together on the same boat to the missions from Spain, and together they served Mission San Miguel.

A fine collection of art, probably the work of José de Paez from Mexico City, is found on the side walls further down the nave. On the left side, from the front, are three paintings of the archangels: St. Michael, St. Gabriel, and St. Raphael. On the right, from the front, are the Paradiso (featuring St. Michael in heaven), St. Anthony of Padua, the Sorrowful Mother, and the Baptism of Christ by St. John the Baptist.

—PRAYER—

We adore You, Lord Jesus Christ, here, and in all your churches throughout the whole world, and we bless You, because by your holy Cross, You have redeemed the world (St. Francis of Assisi).

A READING FROM THE BOOK OF REVELATION:

War broke out in heaven; Michael and his angels fought against the dragon. The dragon and his angels fought back, but they were defeated, and there was no longer any place for them in heaven. The great dragon was thrown down, that ancient serpent, who is called the Devil and Satan, the deceiver of the whole world—he was thrown down to the earth, and his angels were thrown down with him. Then I heard a loud voice in heaven, proclaiming, "Now have come the salvation and the power and the kingdom of our God and the authority of his Messiah, for the accuser of our comrades has been thrown down, who accuses them day and night before our God. But they have conquered him by the blood of the Lamb and by the word of their testimony, for they did not cling to life even in the face of death. Rejoice then, you heavens and those who dwell in them! (Revelation 12:7–12).

V: St. Michael, the Archangel, glorious attendant of the Triune God,

R: Pray for us.

V: Leader of the angelic hosts, Prince of the heavenly armies,

R: Pray for us.

V: Defender of Divine Glory and the Kingship of Christ,

R: Pray for us.

V: Invincible Warrior and Angel of Peace,

R: Pray for us.

V: Guardian of the One, Holy, Catholic, and Apostolic Church,

R: Pray for us.

V: Defender of those who hope in God and Protector of all in danger,

R: Pray for us.

Let us pray:

Most noble Michael the Archangel, guardian of God's people, defend us in battle and deliver us from all enemies, visible and invisible. As we turn to you with confidence, enable us through your protection to serve God more faithfully every day. Obtain for us the grace to live and die in the faith, hope, and charity of the Church, so that we may be eternally united with its Lord, our Savior, Jesus Christ. Amen.

MUSEUM AND GROUNDS

A lily-filled fountain—a replica of the one at Mission Santa Bárbara—forms the focus of the enclosed yard in front of the mission buildings. Twelve arches form the colonnade, each arch of a different size and shape.

Inside the mission buildings, the museum features a statue of St. Michael that dates to the sixteenth century. Other rooms exhibit the life of the Salinan people, models of the mission, daily activities at the mission (including a mission-era wine vat), historical photographs, and religious paintings and artifacts. The living quarters display the kitchen, dining room, bedroom, and *sala* of the padres.

The corridor behind the mission is brightly painted and features the original doors and artifacts from the mission days. The veranda looks out into the lovely landscape of the garden. Connecting this corridor and the front yard of the mission is a narrow passageway that was once a sheepgate. Through this passage, which today displays harnesses and other tools of animal care, the flock of the mission were let out to the pastures and into the quadrangle.

On the other side of the church, the camposanto dates to March 1798, when the first neophyte was buried there. A monument to memorialize the 2,249 Native Americans recorded in the church burial records stands within the grounds.

"Mission of the Sierras"

Founded on July 14, 1771

End of Mission Road

Jolon, CA 93928

www.missionsanantonio.net

Founded by St. Junípero Serra, San Antonio was the third mission of the California chain. The site had been predetermined during the 1769 expedition of Don Gaspár de Portolá, exploring the route from San Diego to Monterey. The area was inhabited by the Salinan people, whose culture was finely tuned to the environment. The place was called the "Valley of the Oaks," set within the picturesque Santa Lucia mountains. The mission's mountainous location has led to its designation as the "Mission of the Sierras."

Serra, along with Fr. Buenaventura Sitjar and Fr. Miguel Pieras, accompanied by soldiers and a few neophytes, set out from Carmel to establish the mission. According to the biography of Palóu, a bell was hung from an oak tree when they arrived at the site, and Serra began ringing the bell vigorously while crying out, "Come, gentiles, come to the holy Church and receive the faith of Jesus Christ." Serra was convinced that he was participating in the Church's call to proclaim the Gospel to the world. "Let me give vent to my heart," he pleaded, "which desires that this bell might be heard all over the world!"[55]

On July 14, 1771, the cross was raised and the founding Mass offered. Noticing that a curious Indian was watching the Mass, Padre Serra declared during the sermon that it was the first time that a gentile had been present at the first Mass of the mission. The Father-President then approached the man and offered him gifts. Serra's gesture bore fruit later in the day when the Indian returned with several of his Salinan tribesmen bearing gifts to exchange. Serra stayed about two weeks after the founding, then left Fr. Sitjar and Fr. Pieras to build the mission.

Because the original site would periodically flood, the mission was moved in 1773 from the original location to its current site, further north in the Valley of the Oaks. In that same year, a small church, workshops, and dwellings were erected of adobe brick. This was also the year in which the first Christian marriage was celebrated in Alta California, joining in matrimony Juan Maria Ruiz, a soldier, and Margaretta de Cortona, a Salinan woman.

Houses of tulles and wood were constructed for the 163 Indian neophytes and soldiers who were part of the mission. A dam was built on the San Antonio River, and three miles of aqueducts and a reservoir system were constructed to bring a reliable water supply to the new location. A gristmill driven by the water system was added later.

Fr. Sitjar stayed at the mission for thirty-seven years and was the guiding hand for the waterworks and much of the construction. He also became fluent in the Telame language, spoken by the local Salinan people, and wrote a grammar and dictionary of the language. He used these to prepare catechisms in the language of the neophytes.

This mission was the first in California to manufacture roof tiles. Shaped over curved wooden forms, the clay was trimmed on the edges, dried in the sun, and then baked in a kiln. These were a great advance over thatch for roofing because they were both fire resistant and water resistant. They protected the buildings from hostile raids and also from the damaging effects of the winter rains. Soon, the red roof tiles were adopted as an element of construction throughout all the missions, and they became a permanent characteristic of California architecture.

The mission was known for the excellence of its music. Fr. Juan Bautista Sancho arrived at the mission in 1804 and remained until his death in 1830. He brought to California some of the first samples of eighteenth-century European music, including sacred plainchant and polyphony, opera excerpts, and instrumental arrangements. He also composed his own work while at the mission; his *Misa en Sol* and *Misa de los Angeles* are among his best. Under his direction, the mission choir and orchestra was known far and wide. In 1814, he wrote the following from the mission:

> The neophytes have considerable musical talent, and they play violins, cello, flutes, horn, drum, and other instruments that the mission has given them... The Indian converts sing Spanish lyrics perfectly, and they easily learn every kind of singing that is taught to them, *canto llano* or plainchant as well as the metric singing of *canto figurado* [and accompanied by instruments]. Also, they can successfully perform as a choir, or even manage to sing a polyphonic Mass with separate, independent melodic lines—as long as there are the necessary performance parts. In all this they are aided by a clear voice and a good ear which they all have, both men and women alike.[56]

Construction of the "great church," as it was called, began in 1810. The adobe walls were six feet thick, and the large ceiling timbers were cut in the mountains and floated to the area on the water of the San Antonio River. Measuring two hundred feet long and forty feet wide, the church was blessed in 1813. The distinctive burned-brick façade and archway, built twelve feet from the front wall of the church and incorporating square towers with bells, was added in 1821. This church formed the basis for the current reconstructed church.

After passage of the secularization laws, Governor Figueroa

signed the proclamation seizing the mission properties and turning them over to the civil authorities. The mission rapidly deteriorated, the Indians were mistreated, and most eventually retreated back to the mountains.

In 1851, Fr. Doroteo Ambris took up residence at the mission, and a few Indian families remained at the mission with him. In 1863, at the recommendation of the US Land Commission, thirty-three acres of mission land was returned to the Church, but by that time, the mission was falling into ruins. In 1882, Father Ambris died at the mission and the mission was abandoned. The valuables and roof tiles were taken by settlers for other constructions, and the adobe buildings were melted until nothing was left except the brick core of the church walls and the arches of its distinctive brick façade.

The early years of the twentieth century saw the beginnings of San Antonio's restoration. The California Landmark League rebuilt parts of the church walls and covered it with a wooden roof. In 1928, the Franciscans returned to minister at the mission, which became an active church again. During the Second World War, the US Army acquired the surrounding area to establish the Hunter-Liggett Military Reservation for the training of troops. The mission's reconstruction was completed in 1952, with funding from the William Randolph Hearst Foundation and the Franciscans of California. It was rebuilt along the lines of its ancient beauty, born anew from its own adobe mud. In 2005, the Franciscan Friars returned the mission to the Diocese of Monterey, which maintains the mission as an active parish and retreat center.

PATRON OF THE MISSION
San Antonio de Padua (St. Anthony of Padua) was born in 1195, thirteen years after St. Francis of Assisi, in Lisbon, Portugal. His parents belonged to one of the prominent families in the city

and gave their son the name of Fernando at his baptism. He felt called at an early age to the religious life and entered the Augustinian order, where he lived a life of intense study and prayer and was ordained a priest in Coimbra.

Then, moved by the martyrdom of five Franciscans in Morocco when their bodies were carried in procession to his monastery, he received permission in 1220 to join the new Franciscan order, where he received the name Antonio. He set out with a desire to serve as a missionary in Morocco, but he became seriously ill. On the voyage back to Portugal, the ship was blown by storms and eastward winds to the coast of Sicily. As his health returned, he attended the great Pentecost Chapter of Mats, attended by three thousand friars in Assisi. Traveling to northern Italy, Anthony soon demonstrated a remarkable ability as a preacher and his fame spread rapidly. His preaching of the Gospel was matched by his holiness and simple lifestyle.

Anthony became the first teacher in the Franciscan order when Francis of Assisi, the order's founder, heard the glowing reports about Anthony and asked him to teach theology to the friars in order to give them a firm grounding in Scripture. Teaching in Bologna, Anthony continued to preach, and he assumed more responsibility within the Franciscan order. In 1226 he was appointed provincial superior of northern Italy and moved to Padua. As his health declined, he preached his last and most famous Lenten sermons. The crowds were so great—sometimes thirty thousand—that the churches could not hold them, so he went into the piazzas or the open fields. People waited all night to hear him, and he needed a bodyguard to protect him from the people armed with scissors who wanted to snip off a piece of his habit as a relic. After his morning Mass and sermon, he would hear confessions, sometimes all day. Anthony died on his way back to Padua on June 13, 1231.

Anthony was a brilliant but humble friar who preached the Gospel with love and courage. When he died, he was only thirty-six years of age and had been a Franciscan but ten years. The following year, Pope Gregory IX declared him a saint. At the canonization, the Pope spoke of him as the "Ark of the Testament" and the "Repository of Holy Scripture." Thus, St. Anthony is often depicted with a burning light or a book of the Scriptures in his hands. In 1946, Pope Pius XII officially declared Anthony a Doctor of the Church. People began praying through Anthony to find or recover lost and stolen articles, remembering a story from his life about how a novice who had decided to leave the community took Anthony's book of Psalms with him. Realizing it was missing, Anthony prayed it would be found or returned to him, and the thieving novice was moved to return the psalter to Anthony and to return to religious life.

The oldest images of St. Anthony depict him preaching in the public square, usually holding a book in his hands. Since the seventeenth century, he is shown most often with the child Jesus in his arms or standing on a book the saint holds. This is traced to a visionary experience involving St. Anthony with the child, and it speaks of the Franciscan sense of wonder at the mystery of Christ's incarnation. For Anthony, like Francis, poverty was a way of imitating the humility and vulnerability of Jesus, who was born in a stable and would have no place to lay his head. Practically every mission of California possesses one or more images of St. Anthony.

MISSION BELLS

The church's distinctive campanario is made of burned bricks, creating its red-checkered appearance. Three bells are hung in the three openings, and the bronze bell that stands in the center is said to be the first bell made in California.

MISSION CHURCH

The layout, design, and colors of the large church interior reflect what it looked like during the mission period. It is lit by shafts of sunlight from the high windows. The walls throughout the church are decorated with the Indian motif of the flowing river of life, and a great painted arch rises over the communion rail. Prominent on the side wall is the pulpit or ambo, where the Gospel is proclaimed and the sermon delivered. The ambo and its cap not only give visibility to the priest but are designed to focus the sound for the congregation.

In the center of the reredos stands a statue of St. Anthony of Padua, the mission's patron. High above stands the Archangel Michael. To the left and right are images of St. Bonaventure and St. Francis of Assisi. All of these statues on the reredos were preserved from the original mission church and were kept in safety when the mission was abandoned. To the left in the sanctuary is a smaller altar dedicated to the Virgin Mary, and to the right is an altar honoring St. Joseph.

On the floor beneath the altar and to the left and right of the altar are five graves of priests who served at the mission. The grave marked "A" is that of Fr. Bueneventura Sitjar, who spent thirty-six years at the mission. He was present with Serra at the founding of the mission and died at the mission in 1808. The grave marked "B" is that of Fr. Francisco Pujol. He came to California in 1795 and died at the mission in 1801. Grave "C" is that of Fr. Juan Bautista Sancho, who served this mission for 26 years and died here in 1830. Grave "D" is that of Fr. Vicente de Sarría, who "died of want and hunger at Mission Soledad" and was brought here for burial in 1835. And grave "E" is that of Fr. Doretéo Ambrís, a priest from Mexico who served the mission after secularization and died here in 1882.

—PRAYER—

We adore You, Lord Jesus Christ, here, and in all your churches throughout the whole world, and we bless You, because by your holy Cross, You have redeemed the world (St. Francis of Assisi).

A READING FROM THE SECOND LETTER OF ST. PAUL TO THE CORINTHIANS:

As we work together with him, we urge you also not to accept the grace of God in vain. For he says, "At an acceptable time I have listened to you, and on a day of salvation I have helped you." See, now is the acceptable time; see, now is the day of salvation! We are putting no obstacle in anyone's way, so that no fault may be found with our ministry, but as servants of God we have commended ourselves in every way: through great endurance, in afflictions, hardships, calamities, beatings, imprisonments, riots, labors, sleepless nights, hunger; by purity, knowledge, patience, kindness, holiness of spirit, genuine love, truthful speech, and the power of God; with the weapons of righteousness for the right hand and for the left; in honor and dishonor, in ill repute and good repute. We are treated as impostors, and yet are true; as unknown, and yet are well known; as dying, and see—we are alive; as punished, and yet not killed; as sorrowful, yet always rejoicing; as poor, yet making many rich; as having nothing, and yet possessing everything (2 Corinthians 6:1–10).

V: St. Anthony of Padua, sanctuary of heavenly wisdom and glory of the Friars Minor,

R: Pray for us.

V: St. Anthony, Ark of the Testament and Repository of Holy Scripture,

R: Pray for us.

V: St. Anthony, example of humility, destroyer of worldly vanity, and lover of the Cross,

R: Pray for us.

V: St. Anthony, zealous for justice, generator of charity, and martyr of desire,

R: Pray for us.

V: St. Anthony, consoler of the afflicted and restorer of lost and stolen things,

R: Pray for us.

V: St. Anthony, guide of pilgrims and deliverer from the snares of the devil,

R: Pray for us.

Let us pray:

O God, who gave St. Anthony of Padua a love for the sacred Scriptures and the gift of teaching them, give us a love for your holy word and a deep desire to encounter you. Through his intercession, help us to find what we have lost and especially to remain in possession of the truest good, peace of spirit and the grace of salvation. Show us, through your saint, what it means to live in Jesus Christ, who humbled and emptied himself for our sakes and the sake of the whole world. Amen.

MUSEUM AND GROUNDS

The extensive museum offers an abundant collection of artifacts and models of mission life. Displays of arrowheads, spear tips, basketry, native foods, medicinal herbs, and pictographs from caves spotlight the indigenous skills of the Salinan Indians. Vestments, religious art, a wooden missal stand, a Spanish chalice and paten, and an original Mass missal with leather binding and metal clasps highlight the religious life of the mission.

Recreations of a typical padre's room and a kitchen display mission life, and a staircase descends to a cool wine cellar, complete with the aromas of wine making. Exhibits of looms and dyes demonstrate the making of textiles, while displays of adobe bricks and mission tiles demonstrate construction. Candle-making apparatus and the bellow and anvils of the blacksmith shop spotlight other trades, and models detail techniques for making olive oil, wine, tiles, and lumber.

The music room features various musical instruments and the teaching methods used. Violins, drums, a mandolin, harp, and flute are among the instruments displayed. The pages of the choir book are made of sheepskin and bound with cowhide using metal clasps. The hand painted on the wall shows the ways musical notation and the scales were taught to the Indians. Called the Guidonian Hand, this system was devised by Guido d'Arezzo, a Benedictine monk and musical theorist of the tenth century. The shapes and colors of notes on the staff indicate the way parts were sung in the mission choir.

The grounds outside offer realistic samples of life in the mission days. The barracks once housed up to six leather-jacketed soldiers. The washing pool, donkey-powered mill, olive-crushing mill, and a threshing floor surround the ruins of the majordomo's house. The tannery vats and the gristmill are seen on the way to the original vineyard, and the boundaries of the 1804 Indian cemetery is found in the direction of the first wheat fields.

On the other side of the property, remains of the aqueduct system lead into the mission from Mission Creek and the San Antonio River, and remnants of the filter house and water reservoir can be seen. The pottery and tile shop shows how dishes, kitchen utensils, and mission tiles were made of clay and fired in a kiln. Floor tiles (*ladrillos*) were made in wooden forms, and the curved roof tiles (*tejas*) were also made using a wooden form before firing. San Antonio seems to be the first mission to have a teja roof. The clay pipes were formed on a potter's wheel. The small ends fit into the large ends so water can flow without leaking.

The grounds also hold two figure heads from sailing vessels, most likely brought to the mission by sailors as thank-offerings to St. Anthony. Seen in the distance is Junípero Serra Peak, a 5,844-foot mountain, the highest mountain in the Santa Lucia Range. The mission includes picnic areas under shade trees to relax and enjoy the peace of this secluded area.

Founded on October 9, 1791
36641 Fort Romie Road
Soledad, CA 93960
www.missionsoledad.com

Fr. Fermín Francisco de Lasuén dedicated this thirteenth mission to Our Lady of Solitude. The site is popularly called Mission Soledad, an apt name for the desolate location. On the first northward expedition in 1769 toward Monterey, Captain Gaspár de Portolá and Fr. Juan Crespí followed the Salinas River. When they camped in this desolate valley and asked the local natives about the area, the only word Fr. Crespí thought he understood was *soledad*, Spanish for loneliness. Two years later, when Fr. Serra passed through the area after founding Mission San Antonio de Padua, he asked an Indian her name and he remembered that the name he heard sounded like *soledad*.

As Fr. Lasuén planted the cross at the mission's founding on October 9, 1791, the solitude was all too evident. There were few natives nearby. Esselen Indians lived in the Santa Lucia Mountains, but they were scattered in villages and isolated from the mission by terrain. The valley was windy, becoming hot and dry during the summer and cold and wet in winter. Conversions were few at first, and building was slow. A peak neophyte population of 687 was recorded in 1804.

The first adobe church was finished in 1797, and the mission began to prosper. The padres tapped the Salinas River to irrigate the wide-spreading fields, and eventually a fifteen-mile aqueduct brought water to the mission from the Arroyo Seco River. Crops flourished and the mission herds began to multiply. The Esselen

Indians told the padres about the healing value of the nearby mineral springs, today called Paraiso Hot Springs, for relief from rheumatism caused by the damp cold.

However, the isolated location and weather extremes limited the length of time any of the padres wanted to stay at the site, and thirty different priests were assigned to the mission during its short life. The only priest to endure the seclusion for any length of time was Fr. Florencio Ibañez, assigned to the mission in 1803. He stayed until his death in 1818, ending a fifteen-year stay as the resident padre, and is buried on the site, the only priest to be buried at the mission. In 1814, the Spanish governor, José Joaquín de Arrillaga, was touring the missions. During his stop at Mission Soledad to visit his friend Fr. Ibañez, he died and, at his request, was buried in a Franciscan habit at the mission.

The Salinas River was both friend and foe during the life of the mission. In 1824, the river rose and destroyed the church. A chapel was built to replace it. In 1828, the river flooded the land and destroyed the chapel. As reconstruction began, another flood in 1832 destroyed what was being rebuilt. Then in 1834 Mexico's Secularization Laws sealed the mission's fate.

The last Franciscan at the mission was the scholarly and amiable Fr. Vicente Francisco de Sarría, a former Father-President of the missions. He authored a medical treatise enti-tled "Descripción de la Operación Cesárea" (1830), the first original California contribution to the field of medicine. In 1835, he fell at the altar while offering Mass and died later that day. The few Indians remaining created a stretcher and carried his body over the long miles to Mission San Antonio de Padua for burial. With his death, the mission was essentially aban-doned for more than a hundred years.

Governor Pio Pico eventually sold the mission remains for eight hundred dollars. Sale of the roof tiles left the walls unprotected from the elements, leading to its nearly complete deterioration. In 1849, J. Ross Browne, a world traveler and reporter wrote: "A more desolate place than Soledad cannot well be imagined. The old church is partially in ruins, and the adobe huts built for the Indians are roofless, and the walls tumbled about in shapeless piles. Not a tree or shrub is to be seen anywhere in the vicinity. The ground is bare, like an open road, save in front of the main building where carcasses and bones of cattle are scattered about, presenting a disgusting spectacle."[57]

In the 1950s, the site began to be restored to life. The Native Daughters of the Golden West sponsored the restoration of the white chapel, rededicated in 1955, and the *convento* wing, opened in 1963. Today visitors can see archeological excavations, the remains of a few mission buildings, and a small museum. The mission chapel is served by the parish church, also dedicated to Our Lady of Solitude, in the town of Soledad. Recently a master plan has been developed to reconstruct and restore the quadrangle buildings.

PATRON OF THE MISSION

The title of Mary, Our Lady of Solitude, refers to the sorrow and loneliness she felt after the crucifixion and death of Jesus, her son, and to her prayerful meditation on the significance of these events. The Virgin of Solitude is a Spanish variation of Nuestra Señora de los Dolores, Our Lady of Sorrows, or Madre Dolorosa. Its devotional origin goes back to Queen Juana, who lamented the death of her husband, Philip I, King of Spain, in 1506.

Powerful representations of the Sorrowful Mother with striking realism are found throughout Spain, beginning in the seventeenth century, especially in Andalusia. The devotion is strongest among those who identify with her sorrows through personal experience. The devotion found ready acceptance in Mexico, and the Feast of Our Lady of Sorrows on September 15 was made universal by papal decree in 1727.

The Seven Sorrows of Mary are a popular devotion, often portrayed by a tearful Mary with seven daggers piercing her heart. Based on the prophecy of Simeon delivered to Mary, "a sword will pierce your own soul too" (Luke 2:25), devotional prayers meditate on each of her seven sorrows. Fine statues and paintings of the Sorrowful Mother, in which Mary is wearing the black or dark blue mourning garments, are found at many of the California missions.

MISSION BELLS

The original mission bell, cast in Mexico City in 1794 by the famous bell maker Ruells, is kept inside the museum. It was kept in storage at San Carlos Mission when the mission was abandoned and then returned to Soledad in June, 1983. A smaller bell now hangs on a wooden beam to the left of the church entrance, where the original bell was rung each day.

MISSION CHURCH

The intimate chapel, not on the site of the original church, evokes the humility of mission life there. The blue-painted ceiling covers the narrow rows of pews. Our Lady of Sorrows, dressed in black lace, looks out into the shadowy chapel from the painted reredos. Above the statue the painting represents the seven piercings of Mary's heart: the prophecy of Simeon, the flight into Egypt, the loss of Jesus in the temple, the meeting of Mary and Jesus along the Via Dolorosa, the crucifixion of Jesus, the piercing of his side and descent from the cross, and his burial in the tomb.

The motif painted along the walls consists of a wavy blue line with yellow dots, representing the river of life carrying souls along the way. A second motif, found on the step leading into the sanctuary, consists of pomegranate flowers, possibly the original design pattern for the church. The fourteen Stations of the Cross are nearly two hundred years old. They were saved from the looting following secularization by being returned to Monterey for safekeeping.

—PRAYER—

We adore You, Lord Jesus Christ, here, and in all your churches throughout the whole world, and we bless You, because by your holy Cross, You have redeemed the world (St. Francis of Assisi).

A READING FROM THE GOSPEL ACCORDING TO ST. JOHN:
Standing near the cross of Jesus were his mother, and his mother's sister, Mary the wife of Clopas, and Mary Magdalene. When Jesus saw his mother and the disciple whom he loved standing beside her, he said to his mother, "Woman, here is your son." Then he said to the disciple, "Here is your mother." And from that hour the disciple took her into his own home (John 19:25–27).

Stabat Mater (thirteenth century)
V: At the cross her station keeping,
Mary stood in sorrow weeping
When her Son was crucified.
R: While she waited in her anguish,
Seeing Christ in torment languish,
Bitter sorrow pierced her heart.
V: With what pain and desolation,
With what noble resignation,

Mary watched her dying Son.
R: Ever-patient in her yearning
Though her tear-filled eyes were burning,
Mary gazed upon her Son.
V: Who, that sorrow contemplating,
On that passion meditating,
Would not share the Virgin's grief?
R: Christ she saw, for our salvation,
Scourged with cruel acclamation,
Bruised and beaten by the rod.
V: Christ she saw with life-blood failing,
All her anguish unavailing,
Saw him breathe his very last.
R: Mary, fount of love's devotion,
Let me share with true emotion
All the sorrow you endured.
V: Virgin, ever interceding,
Hear me in my fervent pleading:
Fire me with your love of Christ.
R: Mother, may this prayer be granted:
That Christ's love may be implanted
In the depths of my poor soul.
V: Fairest maid of all creation,
Queen of hope and consolation,
Let me feel your grief sublime.
R: Virgin, in your love befriend me,
At the Judgment Day defend me.
Help me by your constant prayer.
V: Savior, when my life shall leave me,
Through your mother's prayers receive me
With the fruits of victory.
R: Virgin of all virgins blest!

Listen to my fond request:

Let me share your grief divine.

Let us pray:

O God, who willed that, when your Son was lifted on the cross, his mother should stand close by and share his suffering, grant that we, who remember her sorrows today, may share in his resurrection. Through the intercession of Mary, our Sorrowful Mother, help us to love Christ with true devotion and enkindle our hearts with faith in his saving cross. Show us, through Mary, how to follow him throughout our lives with faith, hope, and love. Amen.

MUSEUM AND GROUNDS

The rebuilt padre's quarters now forms a small museum. The first room is dedicated to the indigenous people. Archaeological evidence shows that the Esselen populated the area for more than four thousand years. Paintings illustrating the area where the natives settled show how the Salinas and Arroyo Seco Rivers often flooded during the winter and spring. In summer the area was dry on the surface, but the underground water produced an abundance of grasses and wildlife that lived off of them. Oak forests ran along the river banks.

Other displays feature Franciscan robes and vestments, keys and a lock, an iron ax, nails, and dueling pistols. A painting depicts the Indians carrying the body of Fr. Sarría some twenty-five miles to Mission San Antonio for burial. Other paintings illustrate the mission in its wind-blown and desolate location.

The Rancho Room shows the period after the mission properties were divided among landowners. The mission buildings were sold to the Soberanes family, famous in the Monterey area for their musical talents and hospitality to visitors passing through. Images of their family members and a copy of the document written by Governor Pio Pico is on display.

The ruins of the original church are at the end of the walkway in front of the museum, on the opposite end of the present white chapel. In the floor of the church ruins are three gravesites. The first marker is that of José Joaquín de Arrillaga, the Spanish governor of California, affectionately known as "Papa." When he died at the mission, he requested to be buried in the church, clothed in Franciscan robes. The second is that of Fr. Florencio Ibañez, who devotedly served the mission for fifteen years until his death. The third gravesite, left anonymous, is that of an Indian woman. The burial of a native woman in such an honorable location is intriguing. She represents all the other unknown native peoples buried at the mission.

The church ruins form one corner of the mission quadrangle, the outlines of which can still be discerned by the broken adobe walls. Signs mark the places where workshops, quarters, and other buildings stood. In the rear courtyard stands a fountain, dedicated to all the people who worked on and are working on the mission's restoration. In back of the courtyard, between the entrance to the grounds and the mission, stands a grove of olive trees. They serve as a reminder that cuttings from Mission Soledad trees were used to build the California olive industry in the mid-1900s. The olive oil produced from these trees is used by the Diocese of Monterey for the sacraments.

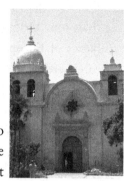

"Father of the Alta California Missions"
Founded on June 3, 1770
3080 Rio Road
Carmel, CA 93923
www.carmelmission.org

The mission was founded by St. Junípero Serra on June 3, 1770, as the second of the California missions. Today it is a monument to the renowned missionary saint, who is buried in the church and whose spirit fills these grounds. Designated as the "Father of the Alta California Missions," Mission Carmel served as the headquarters for all the missions from its founding until 1803, under both Father-President Junípero Serra and his successor, Father-President Fermín Lasuén.

Fr. Serra originally founded the mission on the shores of Monterey Bay along with the presidio. Arriving aboard the *San Antonio*, Serra blessed the ground, hung a bell from an old oak tree, raised the cross, and dedicated the mission to St. Charles Borromeo. Remnants of this landmark oak tree may still be found at the mission museum. Within a year, however, Serra resolved to find a more suitable site for the mission. He found an ideal setting in the beautiful Carmel Valley about five miles away, and the relocated mission was renamed Mission San Carlos Borromeo del Río Carmelo. For the good of the neophytes, Serra wanted to put some distance between them and the Spanish soldiers of the presidio. The new land was also better for agriculture, and there were more native villages located there.

The natives of the area belonged to the Esselen and Rumsen peoples. As they were converted to Christianity, they joined in the construction of the first mission structures, which were made of logs, timber, and brush. Over the next sixty years, more than four thousand were baptized there and were taught the basics of European civilization. They were trained in agriculture, herding, carpentry, and construction. In the early days, the mission was poor and repeatedly faced food shortages. They depended on supply ships, and once were saved by cartloads of bear meat hunted in the Valley of the Bears near present-day San Luis Obispo. But by 1774, the mission began to prosper with increasingly larger agricultural production.

Serra spent the rest of his life with this mission as his home. Although he was continually traveling, making the rounds of the growing missions spread out over five hundred miles, he considered Carmel his center of operations. After more than seventy years of life, worn out from his missionary service, he called his dear friend Fr. Palóu to stay with him and assist his dying. On the day before his death, Serra asked Palóu for the viaticum, the final reception of Holy Communion before death. Serra insisted on going to the church for this ritual. He had also called for the presidio carpenter to prepare his coffin. The Father-President spent his last night on earth in his cell, deep in prayer. He fell asleep in the Lord on the afternoon of August 28, 1784.

Fr. Palóu told the Indians to ring the *doble de campana* with the mission bells to announce the parting of Fr. Serra. The vigil was kept, and the Requiem Mass was offered the next day. The Indian choir provided the music, and hundreds of Indians from every ranchería in the area of Carmel were among the mourners. In the afternoon, a procession was formed, and the officers carried the remains of Padre Serra on their shoulders around the courtyard of the mission. The procession then reentered the church, and the coffin was placed at the foot of the altar.

The open grave was blessed and incensed, then the body of the Father-President of all the California missions was lowered into the sanctuary floor. The lamenting cries mixed with the prayers and chanting of the rite, as all in attendance knew that a saint had passed from their midst.

Fr. Lasuén was named Father-President in 1785, and he directed the construction of the present stone church, which was built by the Indians and dedicated in 1797. During these years, the mission reached the height of its prosperity, as the population of baptized natives reached nearly one thousand and the output from crops was abundant. In 1803, Fr. Lasuén died and was buried beside Fr. Serra.

By the time the mission was secularized in 1834, the native population was greatly reduced due to European diseases. The mission lands were absorbed by the settlers, and the remaining Indian population was dispersed. Gradually the church and quadrangle fell into ruin, as the neglected roof beams rotted and gave way under the weight of the tiles. Although the United States restored the mission property to the local bishop in 1859, it remained at the mercy of vandals and the destructive forces of nature.

It was not until the 1880s that attempts were made to save the historical landmark. Fr. Angel Casanova, the resident pastor in Monterey, decided to open the tombs in the sanctuary to quiet the persistent rumors that Fr. Serra's body had been removed. After the remains were identified and the tombs resealed, Casanova directed that a wooden roof be placed over the mission church, which helped to preserve it.

In 1924, Fr. Ramón Mastres restored the first room of the quadrangle, and more serious restoration began in 1931 when Sir Harry Downie was made curator. He guided the restoration of the mission in every detail for almost five decades and is buried in the mission cemetery. The mission became a parish, and in 1961, Pope John XXIII designated the church as a minor basilica. In 1943, the body of Father Serra was again examined in preparation for his possible canonization, which finally occurred in 2015.

PATRON OF THE MISSION

San Carlos Borromeo (St. Charles Borromeo) was born of noble parents of Lombardi in 1538. His mother was Margherita de' Medici, sister to the future Pope Pius IV. From his youth, Charles was inclined to the religious life. He attended the University of Pavia, where he earned a doctorate in civil and canon law. When his uncle became pope, the twenty-one-year-old was summoned to Rome and made a cardinal and Secretary of State, although he was not yet ordained. He lived a humble, austere life and proved to be a brilliant administrator. He helped to shape many of the reforms of the Council of Trent, and he took a large role in the creation of the Tridentine Catechism, the *Catechismus Romanus*. As a tough and uncompromising personality, he met much opposition to his reforms from secular leaders and clergy.

In 1563 Charles was ordained a priest and, one year later, was appointed Archbishop of Milan. He rid the diocese of many abuses, putting into action the reforms mandated by the Council of Trent. The largest archdiocese in Italy at the time, with more than three thousand clergy and eight hundred thousand people, Milan became a model diocese under his direction. The archbishop founded seminaries for the education of priests, as he believed that inadequate education of the clergy fed much of the laxity that led to the Protestant Reformation. His efforts for catechesis and the instruction of youth were especially fruitful, initiating the work of the Confraternity for Christian Doctrine and the first Sunday School classes. When the terrible plague of 1576 hit the city and the governor and nobility fled,

Charles organized relief efforts for those who were stricken and tended to the dying. Although he was a diocesan priest, he was a member of the Third Order of St. Francis.

Charles Borromeo died in 1584, and his feast is celebrated on November 4. Popular devotion to him arose quickly and continued to grow. In the decades following his death, he was remembered as one of the great reformers of the troubled sixteenth century. He is usually depicted in paintings and sculpture attired as an archbishop or cardinal, with a mitre or cardinal's hat, and a crozier in his hand. Mission San Carlos was named to honor this patron saint of Carlos III, the King of Spain.

MISSION BELLS

The church is crowned with two dissimilar bell towers, the largest with a Moorish-style dome. This tower contains nine bells, some of which were recovered during the restorations of the twentieth century. In 2010, some of the original bells were found to be cracked and had to be recast. The new castings were mounted back in the tower and the originals are on display in the courtyard and museum. An outside staircase leads to this bell tower.

MISSION CHURCH

The sandstone for the church was quarried by Indian laborers under the direction of master stonemasons Manuel Esteban Ruiz and Santiago Ruiz. The walls are five feet thick at the base. The entire façade, especially the bell-towers and the distinctive window over the main door, displays a distinct Moorish design influence. The interior walls taper inward so that the ceiling is formed as an arch.

Beneath the floor of the sanctuary is the tomb of St. Junípero Serra. Next to his tomb lies that of his dear friend and coworker, Padre Juan Crespí, who died two years earlier. Also buried below the sanctuary is Padre Julian Lopez—a young Franciscan at the mission who died the same year the present church was dedicated—and Padre Fermín Lasuén, the second Father-President of the missions, who was buried here in 1803.

On the back wall of the sanctuary, the beautiful reredos displays many images of the saints. At the top, beneath the image of the Holy Spirit, is a statue of St. Charles Borromeo, the patron of the mission. On each side of him are medallions of Sts. Peter and Paul. The central image is the crucified Christ with Mary his mother and John the beloved disciple beneath the cross. To the left are images of St. Michael the Archangel above and Mary the Immaculate Conception below; to the right are images of St. Anthony of Padua above and St. Dominic below.

On the left wall of the sanctuary, next to the sanctuary candle, hangs a painting entitled *Glory of Heaven*, ordered by Fr. Serra from Mexico City and placed in the church in 1774. The painting portrays the Trinity in an unusual way: God the Father is in white and holds the world; the Son is holding the cross; the Holy Spirit is clothed in red. Gathered around them are a number of biblical figures, beginning with Adam and Eve, as well as Mary and Joseph, and numerous martyrs and saints. St. Francis of Assisi kneels on the right, and next to him is St. Dominic, expressing the camaraderie between the Franciscan and Dominican orders. On the opposite wall of the sanctuary hangs a painting entitled *Our Lady of Sorrows*, which was also ordered by Serra and placed in the church in 1778. The painting commemorates Mary's sorrow as she receives the crucified body of her Son. St. John the Apostle and St. Mary Magdalene assist with the corpse of Jesus.

On the right side of the church, next to the sacristy door, a carved wood and glass case contains remnants of the redwood coffin in which St. Junípero Serra's body was originally buried. Above hangs a painting entitled *Serra's Viaticum* by Mariano Guerrero. The oil on canvas was requested by Father Palóu from Mexico City shortly after Serra's death. Viaticum is the Eucharist received in anticipation of death, the spiritual food meant to strengthen the dying person for the journey from this world to eternal life. The painting depicts a moment from the day before the saint's death, when he received Holy Communion from Father Palóu, who is vested in a surplice, stole, and cope, and holding the Blessed Sacrament. Serra is kneeling to the right, with a stole over his Franciscan habit. Around him are friars, soldiers, sailors, and Indians holding lighted candles. At the top of the painting, above the altar and open tabernacle, rests the statue of Our Lady of Bethlehem with the Christ Child in her arms

Further back on the left is a side chapel, the former mortuary chapel, containing the treasured image of *Nuestra Señora de Belén*, Our Lady of Bethlehem. The beautiful statue was brought from Spain and traveled with Serra to the founding of the San Diego mission and later to the dedication of the mission at Monterey. Following the Mass under the oak tree, the congregation sang the Salve Regina in the presence of this image of Our Lady. The statue was soon sent to the Carmel Mission, and, in later years, captains and sailors who navigated the waters of California would often seek the intercession of *Nuestra Señora de Belén* for safe passage. In 1802, the commander of a frigate gave the statue its silver crown in thanksgiving for his ship's safety on a dangerous voyage. The Indians saved the cherished image when the mission was secularized, and their descendant returned it to the church when the mission was restored.

The baptistery at the rear of the church contains the original stone font used in the church from 1797. The painting above the font depicts John the Baptist baptizing Jesus. The hare at the bottom of the scene is a defenseless animal and a symbol of humanity who must put their trust in the hope of salvation given by Christ. Fr. Serra ordered the painting from Mexico City and placed it in the church in 1777. Also toward the rear is the *umbraculum (ombrellone)*, the large umbrella with papal insignia, which designates the church as a minor basilica. In addition, the *tintinnabulum*, also at the rear, is a bell mounted on a pole, also designating the church's status. If a pope were to celebrate Mass in a basilica, both the *umbraculum* and the *tintinnabulum* could be included in the procession. High and deeply recessed windows admit a shadowy light beneath the church's arched ceiling. Along the walls hang paintings of the Stations of the Cross and other devotional images.

—PRAYER—

We adore You, Lord Jesus Christ, here, and in all your churches throughout the whole world, and we bless You, because by your holy Cross, You have redeemed the world (St. Francis of Assisi).

A READING FROM THE GOSPEL ACCORDING TO ST. MATTHEW: Now the eleven disciples went to Galilee, to the mountain to which Jesus had directed them. When they saw him, they worshiped him; but some doubted. And Jesus came and said to them, "All authority in heaven and on earth has been given to me. Go therefore and make disciples of all nations, baptizing them in the name of the Father and of the Son and of the Holy Spirit, and teaching them to obey everything that I have commanded you. And remember, I am with you always, to the end of the age" (Matthew 28:16–20).

V: St. Junípero Serra, who followed the call of the Risen Lord to make disciples of all nations,

R: Pray for us. May we always go forward and never turn back.

V: St. Junípero Serra, who baptized and taught the Gospel to the native peoples of California,

R: Pray for us. May we always go forward and never turn back.

V: St. Junípero Serra, who defended the Indians from violence and abuse,

R: Pray for us. May we always go forward and never turn back.

V: St. Junípero Serra, who endured suffering in imitation of the Crucified Christ,

R: Pray for us. May we always go forward and never turn back.

V: St. Junípero Serra, who served God's people as missionary, pastor, and priest,

R: Pray for us. May we always go forward and never turn back.

V: St. Junípero Serra, who spoke truthfully and humbly against power and injustice,

R: Pray for us. May we always go forward and never turn back.

V: St. Junípero Serra, who teaches us to be missionary disciples of Jesus today,

R: Pray for us. May we always go forward and never turn back.

Let us pray:

Merciful God, who called St. Junípero Serra to preach the Gospel to the peoples of America, inspire us with his apostolic zeal. Through his intercession, protect us in our labor and give us the grace to live our baptismal calling. Help us to take up the cross of your Son Jesus Christ and to be witnesses of the Gospel in the world.

MUSEUM AND GROUNDS

The centerpiece of the museum is the Mora Chapel Gallery, which contains the elaborate Serra Memorial Cenotaph. Created by local artist Jo Mora and unveiled in 1924, the monument is made of travertine marble with life-size figures in bronze. The sculpture of St. Junípero Serra lies atop the monument, his bare feet resting on a reclining bear, a symbol of California, adding a bit of tenderness and whimsy to the solemn scene. The figure of Padre Juan Crespí, who predeceased Serra, stands at the head, praying over him as if to welcome him into the company of the saints. Kneeling at Serra's feet are Padre Julian Lopez and Padre Fermín Lasuén. All of these Franciscans are entombed with the saint beneath the floor of the mission church.

The altar and large gilded cross of the Mora Chapel is adorned with stylized figures of St. Francis of Assisi, St. Charles Borromeo, and St. Anthony of Padua. The chapel also displays rotating art and history exhibitions and paintings of Serra. Above the door hangs the famous image of the founding cere-monies at Monterey Bay, in which Serra offers Mass beneath the famous oak tree with friars, soldiers, sailors, and natives participating. Elsewhere in the museum is a section of this land-mark oak tree, under which Serra dedicated the mission and offered its first Mass.

Displays also contain the story of the canonization of St. Junipero Serra by Pope Francis in 2015. Here is found a small bronze reliquary cross. The cross is a replica of the Caravaca cross, the original of which is in Spain and contains a fragment of the true cross. Serra brought this cross with him when he set out for the New World. At his death, the cross was later placed in his clasped hands and buried with him for a century. Serra's replica contains relics of Blessed Raymond Llull to whom he had a special devotion. Blessed Raymond was a Third Order Franciscan and martyr from Mallorca after whom the Llullian University in Palma was named. Serra was professor of philosophy at the university before receiving his missionary vocation. This cross was placed on the altar at his canonization.

Other rooms of the museum exhibit re-creations of the mission's library, kitchen, dining room, and a simple bedroom and sitting room of the padres. The most moving display is the re-created room in which Padre Serra died. The cell is a sparse and humble setting for the holy death. On the pillow of his bed rests the crucifix that the saint had received in his novitiate and had carried on all his travels. Above his bed hangs the cord of his Franciscan habit, with its three knots representing poverty, chastity, and obedience.

Outside the cell, the hallway displays memories and relics of the saint's life, including the stole placed over his grey habit at his death. The silk, cotton-lined burial stole was taken from Serra's grave by Fr. Casanova in 1882.

The mission quadrangle encloses a large fountain, statues, and flowering plants and trees. A large replica of the cross that Serra erected now rises from the foundation of the original. On the other side of the basilica, the cemetery contains many graves outlined with shells. A cross stands in memory of the Christian Indians and Spaniards who were interred in the cemetery between 1771 and 1833. At the back of the property, behind the basilica, stands a small adobe which houses a small museum describing the life and legacy of the Munras family.

OTHER NEARBY SIGHTS

San Carlos Borromeo Cathedral. When the mission moved to Carmel, the presidio remained, and it remains an active military installation today. The Royal Presidio Chapel is today the San Carlos Borromeo Cathedral. The interior of the cathedral is small and simple, with a high-ceilinged nave and an elegant altar. A section of the oak tree under which Padre Serra offered the Mass of dedication is preserved in the vestibule, and the site of the original "Junípero Oak" is indicated by a marker outside. The grounds also include a shrine to Our Lady of Bethlehem and other garden shrines that invite prayer.

"Mission of Music"
Founded on June 24, 1797
406 2nd Street
San Juan Bautista, CA 95045
www.oldmissionsjb.org

This fifteenth mission was founded by Father-President Fermín Lasuén on June 24, 1797, during that busy summer in which he founded three other missions. The Mutsun people, the original residents of the valley, were friendly and cooperative, volunteering to live at the mission and prepare for baptism. Within six months, they had built not only an adobe church but also residences, barracks, and a granary. The mission grew rapidly and thrived spiritually and materially.

However, the mission was unfortunately built on the San Andreas fault, California's most destructive earthquake zone. While the padres were unable to understand this at the time, the location meant a lot of trembling and unstable days throughout the mission's history. Within a couple of years, the fathers were considering whether to enlarge the church or build a new one, but a series of earthquakes solved the dilemma for them. The cornerstone was laid in 1803, and the elaborate new church was completed in 1812. Although the church was originally designed to have a nave and two side aisles, making it capable of holding more than one thousand worshipers, the padres began to fear that the open-arched walls that separated the aisles from the nave might not support the roof in an earthquake. So they closed in the arches except for those next to the sanctuary, which they left open to form a transept.

The mission especially prospered under the care of two Franciscans. The first, Fr. Felipe del Arroyo de la Cuesta, arrived in 1808 and supervised most of the construction of the church. He was loved by the Indians and had an exceptional talent for languages, preaching in a dozen or more of the native dialects. During his years at the mission, he wrote a compendium of Indian phrases and an exhaustive study of the Mutsun language. The first language he used, however, was cheerful tunes. He had acquired a hand-cranked barrel organ, possibly as a gift from Captain Vancouver, the British explorer. The missionary lugged this instrument out to the Indian settlements, and when he began to crank out the cheerful tunes, his listeners were so delighted that they followed him back to the mission.

The second Franciscan, Fr. Estévan Tápis, arrived at the mission in 1812, after retiring from his work as Father-President of the mission system. He had a special talent for music and taught singing to the Indians, employing a system of notation that used different colored notes to designate different voices. Two of his handwritten choir books are preserved in the museum. Because of his work in teaching music to the natives, especially his famous choir of Native American boys that performed for many visitors, Mission San Juan Bautista has been designated the "Mission of Music."

Music was interwoven into the daily life of the California missions: in liturgy, labor, and recreation. At sunrise, a bell called the people to worship, and families were roused by a morning hymn to the Virgin Mary, "Ya viene el alba" ("Now Breaks the Glowing Dawn"). After Mass all sang the "Alabado," a hymn of praise to God. Christian instruction was provided through the use of hymns, chanted prayers, and basic religious teachings such as the Ten Commandments set to music.

It was the ambition of every Indian family to have a member in the mission choir or orchestra, a *músico*. The music was written for male voices, and often written high enough for boy *tiples* (sopranos) to assist the older contraltos, tenors, and basses. The singing was usually accompanied by instruments, often playing the identical notes sung by the choir, at other times playing short introductions and interludes. The customary instruments were the violin, the viola, the violincello, the bass viol, the flute, the sweet German flute, the trumpet, horns, the *bandola* (lute), the guitar, drums, and the triangle. Besides contributing to the solemnity of Mass and church feast days, these mission orchestras added much to the life and happiness of the Indian village. Eventually almost every mission had a choir and orchestra. These were the first schools of music in California.

Despite periodic damage from earthquakes, the mission was never destroyed. After its secularization in 1835, much of the land was sold to ranchers. The Indians were scattered to other places, many of them working for the new landowners. But the church continued to serve as the local parish, and Mass has been celebrated there continuously from its founding. The town of San Juan Bautista, which grew up around the mission, expanded rapidly during the California Gold Rush. The church was renovated initially in 1884; then in 1949, it was restored to its original design with funding from the Hearst Foundation. Steel beams were hidden in the structure for earthquake protection, and the side aisles were restored. The mission and its grounds were featured prominently in the 1958 Alfred Hitchcock film *Vertigo*, starring Kim Novak and Jimmy Stewart.

PATRON OF THE MISSION

San Juan Bautista (St. John the Baptist) was the son of Zechariah, a priest in the temple of Jerusalem, and Elizabeth, a relative of Mary the mother of Jesus. As a young man, he lived in the wilderness of Judea, perhaps as a member of the Qumran community near the Dead Sea. The Gospels describe John as dressed in camel's hair, wearing a leather belt, and eating locusts and wild honey. In time he began to call crowds of people to a baptism of repentance for the forgiveness of sins.

When Jesus came to the Jordan River, he was baptized by John. On coming up from the waters, Jesus was manifested as the Son of God, and the Spirit of God rested on him like a dove. John the Baptist pointed him out to others, declaring him to be the Lamb of God. John spoke about himself as a prophet, preparing the way of the Lord, but unworthy even to untie the thong of Christ's sandals. John the Baptist was arrested by Herod Antipas and beheaded at the request of Salome, the daughter of Herodias, the wife of Herod.

Images of John the Baptist are found throughout the missions, most often at the baptistery, depicting John baptizing Jesus at the Jordan River as a dove descends from above. He may also be shown accompanied by a lamb, a symbolic reference to Christ as the Lamb of God. The Feast of St. John the Baptist is celebrated on June 24.

MISSION BELLS

The church did not include a campanario. Rather, bells were hung from a wooden bell rack next to the church. The two-tiered campanario with three bells as seen today located by the church entrance was added only in its twentieth-century restoration. At least one of the bells is original.

MISSION CHURCH

A sculpture of John the Baptist, with arms raised to heaven, was installed in front of the church in 2000. This eight-foot bronze, created by Thomas Marsh, depicts John the Baptist as an

Ohlone Indian. This "voice crying in the wilderness" prepares for the coming of the Lord.

The church's wideness can be seen from the inside. The nave and two side aisles make it the largest standing church of the California missions. Its restoration has created a brightly colored and authentic space for worship. Its high ceiling is made of wood, its floor is composed of red tiles, and its columns and arches are painted with organic patterns and rich pigments. The decorated pulpit  mounted high in the nave was the setting for the preaching of Fr. Arroyo. He mastered the Indian tongues better than any other missionary, preaching in all the dialects of the neophytes. Even the stairs leading up to the pulpit are remarkable for their artwork. Fr. Tapis, the retired Father-President of the missions, who had won the hearts of his people through music, died here and is buried under the sanctuary. The place is marked by an engraved stone in the floor.

The colorful reredos and altar were decorated in 1818 by the first American settler of California, Thomas Doak. This sailor from Boston had jumped ship in Monterey and offered to paint the church in exchange for room and board. In the upper three niches, from left to right, are polychrome statues of St. Anthony of Padua, St. Dominic, and St. Francis of Assisi. Below in the center is a life-size image of the patron of the mission, St. John the Baptist. To the left stands a statue of St. Isadore of Madrid, the patron of farmers, and to the right, St. Pascal Baylon, a Spanish Franciscan known for his charity to the poor and afflicted.

The baptistery at the rear of the church was the site of the baptism of countless neophytes. Its two basins are made of sandstone, and an image of John baptizing Jesus hangs behind the fonts. Within the rear side door is carved a "cat door," allowing the cats access at all times to catch mice, a serious pest during the mission times. Within some of the red floor tiles, tracks of small animals can be seen, apparently made while the tiles were still fresh and drying outdoors in the sun.

The orientation of the church and its altar are another feature of this mission. Once a year, just after dawn on the day of the winter solstice, people gather to see an "illumination," a brief but breathtaking interval when a sunbeam shoots through the church's front window to bathe the altar and the sacred objects around it in a blazing patch of light. This had deep meaning for the Indians, integrating their native honor of the sun and earth with their new faith in the Creator of all.

The door on the north side of the church leads to the cemetery. The grounds contain the remains of 4,300 Native American converts and Europeans. The first Christian to die at the mission was Maria Trinidad, buried there April 23, 1798. Beyond the cemetery wall and sloping downward is the original Camino Real, which is also the line of the San Andreas Fault.

—PRAYER—

We adore You, Lord Jesus Christ, here, and in all your churches throughout the whole world, and we bless You, because by your holy Cross, You have redeemed the world (St. Francis of Assisi).

A READING FROM THE GOSPEL ACCORDING TO ST. JOHN:
The next day John saw Jesus coming toward him and declared, "Here is the Lamb of God who takes away the sin of the world! This is he of whom I said, 'After me comes a man who ranks ahead of me because he was before me.' I myself did not know him; but I came baptizing with water for this reason, that he might be revealed to Israel." And John testified, "I saw the Spirit

descending from heaven like a dove, and it remained on him. I myself did not know him, but the one who sent me to baptize with water said to me, 'He on whom you see the Spirit descend and remain is the one who baptizes with the Holy Spirit.' And I myself have seen and have testified that this is the Son of God" (John 1:29–34).

V: St. John the Baptist, prophet of Israel and precursor of the Messiah,

R: May we prepare the way of the Lord.

V: Voice crying in the wilderness, who came in the spirit and power of Elijah,

R: May we prepare the way of the Lord.

V: Calling all to repentance, pointing to Jesus as the Lamb of God who takes away the sins of the world,

R: May we prepare the way of the Lord.

V: Glorious martyr, imprisoned and beheaded for speaking the truth,

R: May we prepare the way of the Lord.

Let us pray:

Lord God, through the preaching and ministry of John the Baptist, you manifested your Son to the world in the waters of the Jordan River. Prepare our hearts for the coming of Christ so that we may trust in him as the Lamb of God who takes away the sins of the world. Through our repentance, may we recognize and work toward the coming of your Kingdom, through Christ our Lord. Amen.

MUSEUM AND GROUNDS

Behind the present church stands the original mission church, today called the Chapel of Guadalupe. In the center, behind the altar, is a portrait of Nuestra Señora de Guadalupe in a gilded frame.

The *convento* wing, which today houses the museum, is all that remains of the mission quadrangle. Here was once the living quarters for the padres and workrooms for the natives. The kitchen once served twelve hundred people three times a day. The rooms of the museum display liturgical vestments, statues, carpentry tools, baskets and arrowheads, clothing, books, maps, and photos.

The musical instruments, choir books, and other musical artifacts are most interesting in this Mission of Music. Two of the music books in the museum were written by Fr. Tapis, with his characteristic colored notation for the choir parts. Several instruments are displayed from the Indian orchestra, which performed both in church and also for village entertainment.

In 1829, Fr. Arroyo reported that Mission San Juan Bautista had received an "órgano de *tres cilindros*." The barrel organ derives its name from wooden cylinders, mounted in a horizontal position and having on its outer surface a number of brass pins. As the barrel revolves by a hand crank, these pins operate a mechanism that allows wind produced by bellows to enter the required pipes. The three *cilindros* (barrels) contain ten tunes each. A list of these tunes is pasted on the side of the case, but some are no longer readable. Those that are clear include "Go to the Devil," "Spanish Waltz," "College Hornpipe," and "Lady Campbell's Reel." Though these are not appropriate music for church worship, these happy tunes must have contributed great pleasure to mission life.

The barrel organ is more than five feet in height, with its two front panels each bearing five ornamental wooden pipes in Gothic design. Inside are seventeen wooden pipes and twenty-nine metal pipes, all of which still sound when the crank is turned. Its inscription indicates that it was made in London in 1735.

Of the many stories told about this barrel organ, one of the best shows its almost hypnotic power. A tribe of warring Tulare Indians swooped down on the mission one day, and the neophytes ran for cover. Fortunately the padre kept his wits, brought out the barrel organ, and began cranking. The neophytes caught on and began to sing with the music at the top of their voices. Their foes were so entranced that they lay down their weapons and demanded more music, even asking to stay so they could continue enjoying the music.

OTHER NEARBY SIGHTS

San Juan Bautista State Historical Park. The town of San Juan Bautista was bypassed by the railroad and lost out to the neighboring town of Hollister (known as "the earthquake capital of the world") in the competition to become the county seat. It is little changed in appearance from a century or more ago, although the taverns, blacksmiths, and other businesses of yore have been replaced by upscale restaurants and antique dealers. Around the mission's historic plaza stand several impressive buildings from the Mexican and American periods, including the Plaza Hotel, the Plaza Hall, and the Plaza Stable. These are maintained as part of the San Juan Bautista State Historical Park, and many of these are outfitted just as they were in the mid-to-late-nineteenth century. The Castro-Breen Adobe, built about 1840, was administrative headquarters for the Mexican government in the area. In accord with the secularization decree, José Castro divided the mission property between friends, relatives, and some former neophytes.

Down a short set of steps to the north of the plaza and the church is a unique place in California. Its dirt trail is both on the original El Camino Real and directly over the San Andreas fault line. The old highway connecting the missions is in more or less its original condition.

Founded on September 25, 1791

126 High Street

Santa Cruz, CA 95060

www.holycrosssantacruz.com

The area along Monterey Bay's northern shore had been inspected and named for the Holy Cross during the 1769 expedition of Gaspar de Portolá. When Father Palóu crossed the San Lorenzo River in 1774, he was impressed by the area and concluded that it would support a successful community. The abundant land was home to the Ohlone Indians, who lived in small groupings throughout the area.

On August 28, 1791, Fr. Fermín Lasuén raised the cross and offered Mass at the site where the mission was to be built. He wrote: "I found the sight to be most excellent as had been reported to me. I found besides, a stream of water very near, copious and important. On August 28, 1791, the [feast] day of St. Augustine, I said Mass and raised the cross on the spot where the mission is to be. Many gentiles came, old and young of both sexes, and showed they would gladly enroll under the Sacred Standard." Then on September 25, 1791, Mission Santa Cruz was formally founded as the twelfth California mission. The event was attended by the Franciscan padres from Santa Clara and the commandant of the San Francisco Presidio.

The first winter, the San Lorenzo swelled and flooded the mission, and the padres had to relocate to higher ground. They rebuilt the mission on the hill overlooking the river. Older missions sent to Santa Cruz a great quantity and variety of gifts. Permanent buildings were quickly erected, and the neophyte population grew. Good climate and fertile soil provided abundant harvests, and, by 1795, the church and mission quad-rangle were complete. Yet, progress was short-lived, as the mission began to experience a relentless series of "hard luck" events.

In 1796, Governor Borica established the Villa de Branciforte, a pueblo for civilian settlers, across the river from the mission, and he expected the mission to support the town. But the first pueblo colonists were a mixed group, including criminals and former Spanish soldiers, who intruded on mission lands and abused the neophytes, causing two hundred Indians to flee the area within two years. The town, with its reputation for lawless-ness and drunkenness, also attracted some neophytes, but the padres imposed severe punishments on those who escaped to the bad influences of the town. Fr. Andres Quintana, who was, by one account, particularly dreadful to wayward neophytes, was ambushed and killed by a group of disgruntled Indians. When they returned his body to his own bed, his death was assumed to be of natural causes. A later investigation in 1812—including the first autopsy in California—led to the conclusion that the priest had been suffocated.

Another blow to the mission came in 1818 when the pirate Hippolyte Bouchard was reported off the Monterey coast. Governor Borica directed Fr. Ramon Olbes to flee with the neophytes to Mission Santa Clara, and he ordered the residents of Branciforte to protect the possessions left at the mission. Instead, the residents of the town stole or destroyed the valu-ables. Throwing a party, they drank the mission wine and looted the church. Although the pirate never attacked, the colo-nists severely damaged the mission and left it struggling and destitute.

In 1834, the mission came to be among the first to be secular-ized. Land was parceled and sold, leaving little of value for the

Indians. The last Franciscan left in 1840, and the mission slowly collapsed due to time and natural disasters. The 1840 earthquake toppled the bell tower, and a second quake in 1857 crumbled the front wall of the church and many of the remaining buildings.

Although the mission no longer existed, the settlements on the former mission lands took the permanent name of Santa Cruz. A wood-framed church was built in 1858 to serve the community. And in 1891, Holy Cross Church, an ornate Gothic-style church was built on the site of the original church. Nearby, a replica of the original mission church, on a scale of one-third its original size, was built in 1932. Today, the church and the mission replica is a parish of the Diocese of Monterey.

PATRON OF THE MISSION

Misión la Exaltación de la Santa Cruz, the full name of the mission, was named after a feast day in the Church calendar that occurs on September 14: The Exaltation of the Holy Cross. The feast celebrates the most predominant symbol of Christianity, the wooden cross on which Jesus was crucified, symbolizing the world's redemption. Paul wrote: "The message about the cross is foolishness to those who are perishing, but to us who are being saved it is the power of God" (1 Corinthians 1:18).This instrument of torture, designed to degrade the worst of criminals, became through Jesus Christ the life-giving tree that saves all people.

At the founding of each of the California missions, a large wooden cross was set up before the offering of the Mass. A large cross was also usually placed in the cemeteries to honor all those buried there. Crosses of wood or iron were often placed on the summit of church façades and towers, and crucifixes were placed on the main altars. Many crosses in side altars and tabernacles were veneered with the iridescent abalone shell, and the neophytes often crafted wooden crosses to hang in their homes.

MISSION BELLS

The bell tower of the original church collapsed in 1840. It contained nine bells, which were sent to Mission Dolores in San Francisco, where they are still in use. At the mission replica of today, a twentieth-century bell hangs in the tower.

MISSION CHURCH

The modest little chapel, about one third the size of the original mission church, does not pretend to duplicate the original. It does contain, however, several statues, paintings, candlesticks, and the tabernacle used when the mission was active. The outside façade proclaims above the doorway, "O Crux Ave Spes Unica" ("Hail O Cross, Our Only Hope"). The bell tower is topped with the Christian symbol that gives the mission its name.

Inside, the simple design features an archway separating the nave and the sanctuary. Above the arch, the stenciled letters read, "Adoramus Te Christe Et Benedicimus Tibi Quia Per Crucem Tuam Redemisti Mundum," which translates "We adore you, O Christ, and we bless you, because by your Holy Cross you have redeemed the world." The altar is flanked by Our Lady of Sorrows on the left and St. Michael, holding his sword and the scales of justice, on the right. Above the altar is St. Joseph holding the Child Jesus.

The Stations of the Cross, accented by simple wooden crosses, stand stark against the white walls. The ceiling above, the windows, and the tile floor below are simple and plain. Gladys

Sullivan Doyle, a long-time resident of the town, contributed all of the construction costs of this replica chapel on the condition that she be allowed to be buried inside. Her grave can be viewed in the baptistery at the rear of the church beneath the bell tower. Here is also found the original baptismal font. It is nicely carved of local limestone.

—PRAYER—

We adore You, Lord Jesus Christ, here, and in all your churches throughout the whole world, and we bless You, because by your holy Cross, You have redeemed the world (St. Francis of Assisi).

A READING FROM THE LETTER OF PAUL TO THE PHILIPPIANS:
Let the same mind be in you that was in Christ Jesus, who, though he was in the form of God, did not regard equality with God as something to be exploited, but emptied himself, taking the form of a slave, being born in human likeness. And being found in human form, he humbled himself and became obedient to the point of death—even death on a cross.

Therefore God also highly exalted him and gave him the name that is above every name, so that at the name of Jesus every knee should bend, in heaven and on earth and under the earth, and every tongue should confess that Jesus Christ is Lord, to the glory of God the Father (Philippians 2:5–11).

V: Holy Cross where the Lamb of God was sacrificed,

R: Save us, O Holy Cross.

V: Tree of death transformed into the tree of life,

R: Save us, O Holy Cross.

V: Hope of Christians and pledge of the resurrection of the dead,

R: Save us, O Holy Cross.

V: Guide of the blind, staff of the lame, and way of those who have gone astray,

R: Save us, O Holy Cross.

V: Restraint of the powerful and consolation of the poor,

R: Save us, O Holy Cross.

V: Refuge of sinners, terror of demons, comfort of the distressed, and hope of the despairing,

R: Save us, O Holy Cross.

Let us pray:

Lord Jesus Christ, who for the redemption of the world gave your life completely even unto death on a cross, we lift up your glorious cross as our sign of salvation. Through your infinite love, you transformed the hated cross, an instrument of humiliation and suffering, into the holy cross, a symbol of victory over the powers of sin and death. For this reason, we wear the holy cross around our necks, hang the cross in our homes, and now sign ourselves with that cross, + in the name of the Father, and of the Son, and of the Holy Spirit. Amen.

MUSEUM AND GROUNDS

The Misión Galeria contains a few items from the mission's earlier days that have survived its struggles. Vestments, prayer books, statues, a piece of the original tile floor, and a chalice used by St. Junipero Serra are exhibited, in addition to modern gifts offered for sale. The room also preserved a painting of the mission by artist Leon Trousset. It was created after the 1857 earthquake and based on details provided by locals. Behind the Misión Galeria, a door leads to a small courtyard with a fountain surrounded by palm and olive trees.

Around the corner from the mission replica is the Santa Cruz Mission State Historical Park. It contains the Neary-Rodriguez Adobe, restored to its original appearance. The austere single-story adobe, built by the Indians, once housed the Ohlone and Yokut families of the mission. The remaining seven rooms (out of the original seventeen) serve as a museum dedicated to various aspects of the mission's history. The rafters of the covered outside veranda reveal the underpinnings of the roof that protected the adobe. Slender willow boughs are bound with leather straps, since iron for nails was hard to come by. Mud and straw cover this construction, which was then topped with curved red tiles to make the building waterproof.

The rooms of the museum feature a scale model of the mission, historical pictures, and displays depicting the lives of the native peoples before and after the missionaries' arrival. One room re-creates the home of a neophyte family, a fire pit in the middle of the room providing light, heat, and place for cooking. Most inhabitants slept on straw mats on the floor, while the lofts were used for storing food.

Another room spotlights everyday labor at the mission. Women's work included washing, culling and grinding grain, sifting flour, spinning yarn, and sewing, while men worked as tanners, shoemakers, farmers, cowboys, weavers, carpenters, blacksmiths, brick-makers, and masons. Histories of the Rodriguez and Neary families narrate the occupation of the adobe after the era of the Franciscan mission.

The yards outside display native plants the Indians used for food and medicine in raised-bed kitchen gardens similar to those the Spanish encouraged the neophytes to create. The patios contain arbors with grapevines and fruit trees, as well as an olive tree and avocado tree. Period kitchen implements are put to use on living history days when visitors can smell bread baking in the beehive oven, cook a tortilla, or dip a candle.

Founded on January 12, 1777
500 El Camino Real
Santa Clara, CA 95053
www.scu.edu/missionchurch

This eighth mission of St. Junípero Serra was founded on the banks of the Guadalupe River in the land of the Ohlone people. From the earliest plans, Mission Santa Clara was to serve as the sister mission to Mission San Francisco de Asís. Viceroy Bucareli's grand design determined that the San Francisco mission and its presidio would protect the mouth of the San Francisco Bay while the Santa Clara mission anchored the South Bay, receiving goods and services meant for the new pueblo at San Jose.

The Santa Clara Valley was an ideal location for a mission, with its fertile land teaming with wild game, ample water flowing year-round, and agreeable climate. It had been praised by the members of the earlier expeditions, including Juan Bautista de Anza, Fr. Juan Crespí, and Fr. Francisco Palóu. The Ohlone people were friendly and generous, living in as many as forty rancherías in the area. Many were drawn to the mission, and, together with Fr. José Murguía and Fr. Tomás de la Peña, they erected a church, residences, granary, and corrals within a year of its founding.

The mission was menaced by floods and had to be moved several times. In 1781, work began on a new adobe church, designed by Fr. Murguía. He worked with the neophytes to erect the most splendid church in the land, but he died four days before Serra arrived from Carmel to consecrate the completed church in 1784. In less than four months, Serra also would follow Murguía in death. The newly constructed mission would become one of the most prosperous in the system, boasting the most baptisms and marriages and the largest neophyte population in the California mission system.

In 1794, Fr. Magin Catalá arrived at the mission, which would be the scene of his missionary labors for the next thirty-six years. He became known as "the holy man of Santa Clara," because of his saintly life and missionary zeal. He fasted and prayed each day, and no labor or journey was too difficult to bring his beloved natives to salvation. He often traveled to distant tribes and returned with natives desiring to join the mission community, having drawn them to the Christian life through his witness. His holiness was marked by the gift of prophecy and other wonders until his death in 1830 in "the odor of sanctity," a fragrant scent marking the bodies of some of the saints.

The third mission church was toppled by an earthquake in 1818. A temporary chapel was then built, which served the community until 1825, when the fifth mission church was built on the site where the present church now stands. The thick adobe walls were richly decorated, and its façade was anchored by a stately bell tower.

The mission and the nearby pueblo of San José experienced friction through the years, as the cattle of the settlers mingled with those of the mission and disputes arose over water rights of the Guadalupe River. In time, the disputes were alleviated through the initiative of Fr. Catalá, who designed an Alameda, a four-mile road connecting the mission with the pueblo. Two hundred Indians planted three rows of willow trees to divide and border this two-way road. The residents of the town of San José would travel the road to Sunday Mass at the mission, wearing brightly colored silks and satins and riding on fine horses and chariots.

Secularization fell on the mission in 1836. The Spanish Franciscans were expelled, and the lands intended for the Indians were quickly sold by civil administrators and the natives dispersed. But before the neglect of the mission became irreparable, it was rescued through the establishment of a Jesuit college on the land in 1851, the first college of higher learning in the new state of California.

Ten years after the founding of the college, Burchard Villiger, SJ, began a rebuilding campaign to upgrade and enlarge the campus. A devastating fire in 1926 destroyed the mission church, which was then rebuilt in a neo-colonial style with a reconstructed bell tower. The new church was more than twice as wide as the 1825 structure, and the original adobe was replaced with steel-reinforced concrete. Today the mission church serves as the center and heart of Santa Clara University.

PATRON OF THE MISSION

Santa Clara de Asís (St. Clare of Assisi) was born of noble parents in the Umbrian region of central Italy in 1194. Refusing to marry a wealthy suitor chosen by her father, she was attracted to the lifestyle of Francis of Assisi. At the age of eighteen, she heard Francis preach a Lenten sermon and then asked him to help her to live the life of the Gospel. On the evening of Palm Sunday in 1212, Clare left her father's house and proceeded to the Porziuncula, the chapel of Francis and his followers. There her hair was cropped and she exchanged her gown for a plain robe and veil. At first she went to a convent of Benedictine nuns, but in 1215, she moved to a small dwelling that was built for them next to the church of San Damiano, which Francis had repaired some years earlier.

Clare was joined by other women, and they were known as the Poor Ladies of San Damiano. Clare's mother, Ortolana, belonged to a noble family and was a devout woman who had undertaken pilgrimages to Rome, Santiago de Compostela, and the Holy Land. Later in life, Ortolana entered Clare's monastery, following the entry of Clare's sisters, Beatrix and Agnes. As the Second Order of St. Francis, they lived a simple life of poverty, austerity, and seclusion from the world. For a short period, the order was directed by Francis himself, then in 1216, Clare accepted the role of abbess of San Damiano. Clare defended her order from the attempts of prelates to impose a rule on them that more closely resembled the Rule of St. Benedict than Francis's stricter vows. Clare sought to imitate Francis's virtues, played a significant role in encouraging and aiding him, and took care of Francis during his final illness.

After Francis's death, Clare continued to promote the growth of her order and wrote a rule for her community. In 1224, the army of Frederick II came to plunder Assisi. Clare went out to meet them with the Blessed Sacrament in her hands. Suddenly a mysterious terror seized the enemies, who fled without harming anyone in the city. She wrote letters to abbesses in other parts of Europe and four famous letters to Agnes of Prague. Until her death, she thwarted every attempt to compromise the radical commitment to corporate poverty she had originally embraced.

Clare died at San Damiano on August 11, 1253, and was canonized in 1255. Ten years after her death, the name of the order was changed to the Order of St. Clare, popularly known as the Poor Clares. The Basilica of Santa Chiara was built in her honor in Assisi, and her relics are venerated in the crypt today. She is usually depicted in statues and paintings with her brown habit, holding the staff of an abbess and a monstrance with the

Blessed Sacrament. Along with St. Francis, she is considered the cofounder of the Franciscan movement, which has renewed the Church for more than eight centuries.

MISSION BELLS

The bell tower houses three bells that date to the mission period. The oldest two were gifts to the mission from King Carlos IV of Spain, dated 1798 and 1799. A fourth bell, donated in 1929 by King Alphonso XIII of Spain, is now displayed at the De Saisset Museum on the university campus.

MISSION CHURCH

In front of the church is the tall mission cross. Encased within its base is a portion of the original founding cross of 1777. The façade of the church is classically Spanish, and the entire university campus beautifully matches the color and style. The three statues on the façade are bronze replicas of the earlier pear wood statues carved in Oberammergau, Germany. St. Clare stands in the center, with St. John the Baptist and St. Francis to her left and right. In the vestibule, three dates are etched into the tile floor: 1777, the founding date of the mission; 1822, the relocation to the present site; and 1928, the dedication of the present church. The nave is flanked by seven side chapels and painted in shades of yellow, green, blue, and red.

In the sanctuary, the ceiling and reredos are replicas of the 1825 church. In the center stands St. Clare, holding the Blessed Sacrament and her abbess's staff. To her left and right are the Virgin Mary and St. Joseph. Above them is St. Michael the Archangel, and the oval paintings to his left and right are of Sts. Francis and Dominic. The large wall paintings on either side of the reredos, painted by Candelario Rivas in 1931, represent St. Francis at the foot of the cross and St. Anthony of Padua with the Christ child. On the left and right side of the archway dividing the sanctuary from the nave are mission-era statues of St. Gertrude and the Virgin Mary. The frescoed ceiling reproduces Augustin Dávila's Heavenly Court.

To the right of the sanctuary along the north wall, the chapel holds a life-size crucifix, carved in Mexico and brought to the mission in 1802. This precious statue, saved from the 1926 fire, is called the Catalá crucifix, because the saintly Franciscan prayed day and night before this image. Two witnesses testified that they saw the beloved missionary raised from the floor during prayer and embraced by Christ from the cross. To the left of this chapel is the headstone for Fr. John Nobili, SJ, the founder of Santa Clara College.

The next chapel is dedicated to St. Ignatius of Loyola, the founder of the Jesuit order. To the left of the chapel is the headstone for James Murphy, son of the pioneer family that founded the city of Sunnyvale and one of the first students to attend Santa Clara College. The next chapel honors St. Anthony of Padua. On the side hangs a portrait of St. Cajetan, an Italian church reformer and contemporary of St. Ignatius. The last chapel on this side holds a painting of the Holy Family of Jesus, Mary, and Joseph juxtaposed with God the Father, Son, and Holy Spirit, painted in 1889 by Riva Giuseppe Bergamo.

On the left side of the church, the first altar from the rear holds a mission-era statue of St. Francis in the center, along with images of St. Collette and St. Francis of Solano, all saved from the 1926 fire. The display within the reredos holds a relic of St. Junípero Serra. The next chapel honors St. Joseph. It is also the original site of Fr. Catalá's bedroom, since the current church is much wider than the original and the padre's wing attached to the previous adobe church. The next chapel is dedicated to Our Lady of Guadalupe and holds a reproduction of the miraculous image imprinted on the serape of St. Juan Diego, canonized in 2002. Above is the much older painting of Our Lady, Refuge of Sinners, along with two statues of the parents of Mary, Sts. Joachim and Anne, all works of art thankfully saved from the 1926 fire.

—PRAYER—

We adore You, Lord Jesus Christ, here, and in all your churches throughout the whole world, and we bless You, because by your holy Cross, You have redeemed the world (St. Francis of Assisi).

A READING FROM THE SONG OF SONGS:
My beloved speaks and says to me:
Arise, my love, my fair one,
and come away;
for now the winter is past,
the rain is over and gone.
The flowers appear on the earth;
the time of singing has come,
and the voice of the turtledove
is heard in our land.
The fig tree puts forth its figs,
and the vines are in blossom;
they give forth fragrance.
Arise, my love, my fair one,
and come away (Song of Songs 2:10–13).
V: St. Clare, vessel of holiness, lover of chastity, and chosen of Christ,
R: Pray for us.
V: St. Clare, prayerful imitator and daughter of St. Francis,

R: Pray for us.

V: St. Clare, Consecrated light of sanctity and humble follower of Christ,

R: Pray for us.

V: St. Clare, mother and foundress of the Poor Clares,

R: Pray for us.

V: St. Clare, full of joy, poor with the poor, rich in merit and grace,

R: Pray for us.

V: St. Clare, seraphic adorer of the Blessed Sacrament and protector of Assisi,

R: Pray for us.

V: St. Clare, mirror of patience in suffering and comforter of the ill and dying,

R: Pray for us.

Hear this blessing of encouragement from St. Clare of Assisi:

Place your mind before the mirror of eternity!

Place your soul in the brilliance of glory!

Place your heart in the figure of the divine substance!

And transform your entire being into the image of the
  Godhead Itself

through contemplation.

So that you too may feel what His friends feel

as they taste the hidden sweetness

which God Himself has reserved

from the beginning

for those who love Him. Amen.[58]

MUSEUM AND GROUNDS

To the right of the church is a rose garden within the original cemetery. Thousands of Ohlone, Spaniards, Californios, and Anglos were buried there from 1822 to 1851. Hugging the left side of the church is a long wooden arbor hung with wisteria. The trunk measures six feet around and is more than 130 years old.

In the mission gardens are remains of the original mission quadrangle, and bordering the garden is a freestanding adobe wall, erected in 1822. The former living quarters of the padres extended from this wall to the left altars within the church. Behind the gardens stands the Adobe Lodge, originally part of the mission quadrangle. Today it is used for faculty dining and receptions. The nearby Sacred Heart statue sits atop the site of the old mission well.

Directly in back of the church and next to the mission office is the small St. Francis Chapel, which holds the last remains of the original mission church's adobe wall and floor.

OTHER NEARBY SIGHTS

Santa Clara University. The campus of Santa Clara University is nicely landscaped and beautiful when in bloom. When the university is in session, students study and relax on the soft lawns. The De Saisset Museum on the university campus is worth a visit, especially the California History Exhibit on the lower level.

Founded on June 11, 1797

43300 Mission Boulevard

Fremont, CA 94539

www.missionsanjose.org

In 1795, Father-President Fermín de Lasuén urged the Spanish viceroy to establish five new missions to fill in the gaps between those already created. He shrewdly suggested that establishing missions no more than a day's journey apart would save the royal treasury the expense of providing military escorts for supply caravans as they stopped overnight along the desolate trails.

Expeditions were sent out from several places along El Camino Real, each accompanied by a missionary who kept a journal of the trip. The expedition that departed from Santa Clara traveled northeast to a site east of the San Francisco Bay, setting up a cross on an elevation near Alameda Creek. When permission was received from the authorities, Fr. Lasuén set out with the founding team to the site, and on Trinity Sunday, June 11, 1797, he blessed the cross and offered Mass, dedicating the fourteenth mission.

The mission was established in the land of the Ohlone people, a site with flowing water and good soil. Although only thirty-three Ohlone entered the mission the first year, the population would eventually include nearly two thousand neophytes. After the construction of temporary shelters, a herd of several hundred cattle and a sizable flock of sheep were donated from the nearby missions. Eventually it became the agricultural and livestock powerhouse of the northern missions, with records in

1832 documenting a herd of 12,000 cattle, 11,000 sheep, and 1,100 horses.

Fr. Buenaventura Fortuni and Fr. Narciso Durán arrived at the mission in 1806 and were largely responsible for its great success. They would serve together for twenty years, with Durán staying a total of twenty-seven years. Fr. Durán was an accomplished musician and adept at teaching others. Obtaining classical instruments from Mexico, he taught the Indians to read music and play a variety of instruments. Then he organized the legendary mission orchestra and choir. Indians would walk many miles to hear one of their concerts.

Success at the mission was clouded by neophyte discontent. A Yokut Indian, baptized with the named Estanislao and educated in the mission system, became a favorite of Fr. Durán and was appointed a mission supervisor. But the free life of the wilderness tempted him and, in 1828, he led a revolt of natives against the Mexican government in order to halt further intrusions into their ancestral homelands. The rebels raided settlers, stole horses, defeated soldiers, and eluded capture. He was joined by Chumash Indians and other Yokuts until at one time his band included almost a thousand men. Estanislao educated them in battle techniques he had learned from Spanish and Mexican soldiers. His raids on civilian settlers usually involved a sudden trap, ending with no loss of life. Instead, he would use his sword to carve his initial, "S," confirming his work. Finally, defeated by the Mexican army, Estanislao returned to the mission and sought the protection of Durán, who helped him secure a pardon. He spent the last years of his life at the mission, teaching others the Yokut language and culture. Stanislaus River and County today are named after this native freedom fighter.

Secularization was carried out in 1836. The Spanish priests were replaced by a Mexican missionary, who was put in charge of the church, while the remainder of the mission land was placed under the supervision of José de Jesús Vallejo. As was the usual practice, the mission lands intended for Indian ownership were sold by Mexican governor Pio Pico to wealthy Californios.

The 1809 adobe church lasted until an earthquake in 1868 irreparably damaged it. A wooden Gothic-style church was then built on its foundation to serve the needs of the parish. In 1982, the old St. Joseph Church was removed and carefully relocated to Burlingame. Then, guided by drawings and historical accounts, architects, archeologists, and volunteers began an authentic reproduction of the original mission church from adobe bricks and tiles, using historical tools and materials. The result is an impressive testimony to the mission heritage.

PATRON OF THE MISSION

San José (St. Joseph), spouse of Mary and adoptive father of Jesus, lived in Nazareth and had ancestral roots in Bethlehem. He is prominent in the infancy accounts of the Gospels of Matthew and Luke. He is described as a just and righteous man, and as one whose trade was that of a *tekton* (in Greek), a craftsman who is skilled in working in stone, masonry, and wood. The Gospels describe him as a descendant of King David.

When he came to know that his betrothed was carrying a child, he decided not to expose her—in order to protect her from the imposition of the usual penalties—but to quietly divorce her. But when it was revealed to him that Mary was bearing the Son of God, he immediately took her as his wife. With diligence and love, he sought shelter for his wife in Bethlehem when she was about to give birth, and later he led his family to Egypt as refugees from the plotting of Herod. As a faithful Jew, he taught his son the traditions of Israel and taught him his own trade. Christian tradition holds that Joseph must have died before the public ministry of Jesus, because he is not mentioned in those accounts.

St. Joseph is most often depicted holding the Christ child and a staff from which buds have blossomed. The flowering staff is rooted in the messianic prophecy of Isaiah concerning the descendant of King David: "But a shoot shall sprout from the stump of Jesse, and from his roots a bud shall blossom" (Isaiah 11:1; also Isaiah 27:6). His feast day is celebrated on March 19. He is the patron of fathers, husbands, and workers, and the protector of the universal Church. Pope Francis advised that St. Joseph be mentioned in the Eucharistic Prayer of every Mass.

MISSION BELLS

The bell tower is quite truncated because of the fear of earthquakes. In fact, when the earthquake hit in 1868, the bells fell out of the turret that held them. The reconstructed bell tower was completed in 1985, and today it holds the four original bells from the mission era. Two may be seen from the front and two from the side of the belfry.

MISSION CHURCH

This authentic reconstruction of the original adobe church of 1809 is accurate in all its details, and the interior appears now as it did after being redecorated in the years 1833–1840. Front and center above the altar is a fifteenth-century Spanish statue of St. Joseph, patron of the mission. He is holding a blossoming staff and the Christ child. Above is an oval painting of Christ, and above him is a dove representing the Holy Spirit and God the Father. The smaller ovals on each side depict the Holy Family and the Crucifixion. Beneath the image of St. Joseph is a statue of Mary, carved in eighteenth-century Mexico. The large silver candle holders are actually made of wood, painted silver.

The spacious nave contains a simple tile floor and white walls decorated with columns, ribbons, and balconies, all recreations of the original design of Agustín Dávila. The altar on the left wall near the sanctuary features a statue of St. Bonaventure that survived the 1868 earthquake. The tabernacle door, depicting John the Baptist pointing to the Lamb of God, is a seventeenth-century piece from Guatemala. Further down the left wall, near the entrance, the altar features an image of Christ after his scourging, as he was presented to the crowd by Pontius Pilate. This statue also survived the earthquake. Beneath the image are relics of Roman martyrs and a nail said to contain filings from a nail of the true cross within its hollow center. The entire altar honors the Christian martyrs of the past and present.

The lovely organ in the loft today is the fulfillment of the dream of Fr. Durán, who during his tenure requested, but never received, an organ. At the back of the church stands the baptismal font from the 1830s. It is made of hammered copper with a wooden pedestal. Nearby in the floor is the grave of Robert Livermore (1799–1858). Many prominent Spaniards were buried in the church, but only the grave of Livermore was marked and discovered after the earthquake. A rancher and landowner, his holdings eventually formed the basis of the city that bears his name. On the right wall, near the sanctuary, a statue of St. Joachim is free-standing without an altar. He is honored as the father of the Virgin Mary. Near the statue is a bronze plaque commemorating the restoration of the church: "The Bells Shall Ring Again."

—PRAYER—

We adore You, Lord Jesus Christ, here, and in all your churches throughout the whole world, and we bless You, because by your holy Cross, You have redeemed the world (St. Francis of Assisi).

A READING FROM THE HOLY GOSPEL ACCORDING TO ST. MATTHEW:

Now the birth of Jesus the Messiah took place in this way. When his mother Mary had been engaged to Joseph, but before they lived together, she was found to be with child from the Holy Spirit. Her husband Joseph, being a righteous man and unwilling to expose her to public disgrace, planned to dismiss her quietly. But just when he had resolved to do this, an angel of the Lord appeared to him in a dream and said, "Joseph, son of David, do not be afraid to take Mary as your wife, for the child conceived in her is from the Holy Spirit. She will bear a son, and you are to name him Jesus, for he will save his people from their sins." All this took place to fulfill what had been spoken by the Lord through the prophet: "Look, the virgin shall conceive and bear a son, and they shall name him Emmanuel," which means, "God is with us." When Joseph awoke from sleep, he did as the angel of the Lord commanded him; he took her as his wife, but had no marital relations with her until she had borne a son; and he named him Jesus (Matthew 1:18–25).

V: St. Joseph, spouse of the Virgin Mary and protector of the Holy Family,

R: Pray for us.

V: St. Joseph, adoptive father of Jesus, who gave to Jesus his lineage from King David,

R: Pray for us.

V: St. Joseph, righteous man of Israel, man after God's own heart,

R: Pray for us.

V: St. Joseph, traveling to Bethlehem with Mary your spouse,

R: Pray for us.

V: St. Joseph, bearing in your arms the Son of God,

R: Pray for us.

V: St. Joseph, fleeing into exile with Mary and Jesus,

R: Pray for us.

V: St. Joseph, seeking your child in Jerusalem and finding him in the temple,

R: Pray for us.

V: St. Joseph, witnessing the hidden life of Jesus and dying in the arms of Jesus and Mary,

R: Pray for us.

V: St. Joseph, patron and inspiration for husbands and fathers,

R: Pray for us.

V: St. Joseph, model for workers, consecrating the labor of your hands to God,

R: Pray for us.

V: St. Joseph, in all our homes, in all our afflictions, in the hour of death, and in the day of judgment,

R: Pray for us.

Let us pray:

Almighty God, who gave to the just man from Nazareth, St. Joseph, the privilege of serving as earthly Father to Jesus your Son, through his intercession watch over our families and guide us in your ways. May this son of David, in whom the shoot from the stump of Jesse has blossomed, guide your people with care and protect your Church from harm. United with Mary his spouse and Jesus our Lord, may we be joined forever in the joys of your heavenly kingdom.

Museum and Grounds

The door on the left side of the church nave leads to the cemetery. Above the doorway on the outside, a skull and crossbones mark the way. A plaque notes that many pioneers of the mission era, including Native Americans, Mexicans, and Spaniards, rest here. Graves at that time were marked with small wooden crosses, if marked at all, so the large monuments here are mostly from the late nineteenth century, after the mission period.

Originally the *convento* connected to the church. The stone foundation between the church and the museum is being preserved for future reconstruction. The garden area and patio area include a small fountain and a statue of St. Junipero Serra.

The rooms of the museum depict the history of the mission, beginning with the Ohlone people before the arrival of Europeans. This hunting and gathering culture thrived on the shores of the San Francisco Bay and the Monterey Bay. The displays include ceremonial items, musical instruments, tools, hunting gear, and finely woven baskets. The mission-era displays include a typical padre's room, vestments and items used for Mass, and a page from the choir book created by Fr. Durán, as well as instruments used in his orchestra. Other rooms present life for the settlers after the mission's secularization and details of the mission's reconstruction and restoration.

"Mission Dolores"

Founded on June 29, 1776

3321 Sixteenth Street

San Francisco, CA 94114

www.missiondolores.org

Located today in the heart of San Francisco's Mission District, the mission is the oldest intact building in the city. The sixth of the California missions, the settlement was named for St. Francis of Assisi. But it was also commonly known as Mission Dolores, owing to the presence of a nearby creek named Arroyo de Nuestra Señora de los Dolores (Our Lady of Sorrows Creek).

The European discovery of San Francisco Bay had been made by Spanish explorers in 1769, under the direction of Gaspar de Portolá. Then in 1775, Juan Bautista de Anza began an epic journey from Mexico with 240 soldiers, settlers, and natives to establish a site for a presidio and a mission at the bay of San Francisco. In 1776, the exploring party planted a cross on the white steep rock overhanging the Golden Gate, the location of which is today's Fort Point. Fr. Pedro Font, who blessed the cross that day, wrote the following in his diary:

> Indeed, although in my travels I saw very good sites and beautiful country, I saw none which pleased me so much as this. And I think that if it could be well settled like Europe there would not be anything more beautiful in all the world, for it has the best advantages for founding in it a most beautiful city, with all the conveniences desired by land as well as by sea.[59]

After surveying the area, Anza selected the site for the future mission near a spring and lagoon, which he named *Nuestra*

Señora de Los Dolores, because it was the feast day of Our Lady of Sorrows. The founding expedition then left Monterey. It was made up of some fourteen soldiers, seven settlers, Fr. Francisco Palóu and Fr. Pedro Benito Cambón, thirteen young Indians, plus women and children. They were accompanied by a large mule train and a herd of 286 cattle. Indians they met along the way were amazed at the number of people and fascinated by the cattle, since they had never seen these before. The party was welcomed along the way, and they made camp near the seasonal Indian village of Chutchui along Arroyo de los Dolores.

Although the mission was founded under the presidency of Fr. Serra, he was not present at its first Mass on June 29, 1776. This was offered by Serra's student and friend, Fr. Francisco Palóu. At this same time, on the opposite coast of North America, Thomas Jefferson, John Adams, and Benjamin Franklin were working on their draft of the Declaration of Independence, to be promulgated five days later.

The mission was formally inaugurated on October 9. The first church was made of thatch, mud, and logs. A statue of St. Francis was processed and placed on the altar, Mass was celebrated, and the mission bells pealed forth. The church that stands today was erected mostly by neophytes between 1782 and 1791. The quadrangle would eventually encompass residences, a school, a girl's dormitory, workshops, soap works, a tannery, mills, and storerooms. A measles epidemic struck in 1795, killing large numbers of Indians, and many fled the mission in its aftermath. The disease couldn't be controlled, but was no doubt exacerbated by the cold and fog that blankets San Francisco year round.

When the Mexican government ordered the mission to be secularized in 1834, the church was placed in the care of a diocesan priest. The coming of the Americans, especially the

forty-niners looking for gold, caused an explosion in the population of San Francisco. The mission area became a resort and
entertainment district, and mission properties were used for
saloons, gambling, racetracks, and bull-and-bear fights. Yet at
the same time, the parish expanded, and a larger church in the
Gothic Revival style was built next to the old mission church
and dedicated in 1876 on the hundredth anniversary of the
mission's founding.

The San Francisco earthquake of 1906 rocked the city and
caused a great fire. It damaged the large church to the extent
that it had to be raised, but the adobe mission church was
spared when the fire advanced no further. Construction began
again on the large Gothic church and was completed in 1918.
This church became known as Mission Dolores Basilica in
1952, when it was designated a minor basilica by Pope Pius XII.

PATRON OF THE MISSION

San Francisco de Asís (St. Francis of Assisi) was born in 1181
in the Umbria region of central Italy. As the son of a wealthy
cloth merchant, Francis lived a frivolous youth and fought as a
soldier for Assisi. Captured and imprisoned, he lost his taste for
the worldly life. He began caring for lepers, and on a pilgrimage
to Rome, he joined the poor in begging.

Returning to Assisi, he had a mystical vision in the chapel of
San Damiano, just outside of Assisi, in which the icon of the
crucified Christ said to him, "Francis, go and repair my house,
which is falling into ruins." He took this to refer to the ruined
church in which he was praying, so he sold some cloth from his
father's store to assist the priest there for this purpose. In the
midst of legal proceedings before the bishop of Assisi, Francis
renounced his father, publicly laying aside even the garments he
had received from him. Returning to the countryside around
the town for two years, he embraced the life of a penitent,

during which he restored several ruined chapels, among them the Porziuncola, the little chapel of St. Mary of the Angels just outside the town, which has become the spiritual heart of the Franciscans.

Francis began to preach on the streets and gathered followers. He founded the men's order of Friars Minor, the women's order of St. Clare, and the Third Order of St. Francis for men and women. In 1219, he went to Egypt in an attempt to convert the Sultan and to put an end to the conflict of the Crusades. In 1224, he received the stigmata, making him the first recorded person to bear the wounds of Christ's Passion. While ill and being cared for by Clare and her sisters at San Damiano, Francis composed the Canticle of the Creatures, praising God for the unity of all creation. He died during the evening hours of October 3, 1226, and is buried in the basilica dedicated to him in Assisi.

St. Junípero Serra and the early missionaries of California were all members of St. Francis's Order of Friars Minor. When the Father-President was working out the details of the first missions with Inspector-General Galvez, Serra asked why there was no mission planned to honor the founder of his order. And Galvez facetiously replied, "If St. Francis wants a mission, let him cause his harbor to be discovered and it will be placed there." Because of its narrow entrance, the bay had escaped the scrutiny of passing vessels, and overland explorers only came upon it in 1769. So, San Francisco soon became the patron of the bay, the mission, the presidio, and subsequently of the great city, all of which bear his name.

MISSION BELLS

The three original bells hang in narrow niches above the entranceway to the church. The first was cast in 1792 and presented to the mission by Viceroy Mendoza. Two larger bells—dedicated to San Francisco, San Jose, and San Martin—are dated 1797. Although they were originally designed to swing, they are now stationary, bolted and lashed in place with rawhide. They are still rung today, operated by cords from the church floor.

MISSION CHURCH

Surviving earthquakes, fires, and other disasters, the church is the oldest intact mission church in California. The original redwood supporting the roof remains in place. The ceiling, although restored, depicts the original native designs of the Ohlone in gold, red, silver, and white. The arch over the sanctuary was painted with a red foliage design, including the symbol IHS, a contraction of the Greek name for Jesus, and MA, the symbol for Mary. The church retains the red tile floor on which the original neophytes knelt in worship.

The gilded reredos behind the main altar came from San Blas, Mexico, in 1796. Probably crafted in Spain and used in an older church in Mexico, the elaborate altarpiece was transported in sections on the backs of mules and oxen. Its original pigments, stains, gold leaf, and lacquer are still apparent. At the top center is a statue of St. Michael the Archangel; on the left are a small statue of St. Francis in Ecstasy and a larger image of St. Joachim, the father of Holy Mary; and on the right are an image of St. Clare of Assisi and a small statue of St. Francis with the stigmata. Below, to the left of the crucifix, is a statue of Holy Mary of the Immaculate Conception and, to the right, a statue of St. Anne, the mother of Mary.

The two side altars face each other and are both decorated with gold leaf, their wooden columns painted to imitate marble.

All of the statues of the saints date from the mission times. On the left side, when facing the main altar, are representations of St. John of Capistrano, OFM, St. Joseph, and St. Bonaventure OFM. On the right side stand statues of St. Pasqual of Baylon, OFM, St. Anthony of Padua, OFM, and St. Francis of Solano, OFM.

The choir loft was originally accessed by way of an outside stairway, and the present spiral staircase is a later addition. What looks like two swinging doors at the back of the church is a confessional. When these panels are swung out from the wall, they form two screens, with a place for the priest to sit between them. The baptistery was the sight of thousands of baptisms, all still recorded in the baptismal register found in the museum.

—PRAYER—

We adore You, Lord Jesus Christ, here, and in all your churches throughout the whole world, and we bless You, because by your holy Cross, You have redeemed the world (St. Francis of Assisi).

A READING FROM THE LETTER OF ST. PAUL TO THE PHILIPPIANS: More than that, I regard everything as loss because of the surpassing value of knowing Christ Jesus my Lord. For his sake I have suffered the loss of all things, and I regard them as rubbish, in order that I may gain Christ and be found in him, not having a righteousness of my own that comes from the law, but one that comes through faith in Christ, the righteousness from God based on faith. I want to know Christ and the power of his resurrection and the sharing of his sufferings by becoming like him in his death, if somehow I may attain the resurrection from the dead. Not that I have already obtained this or have already reached the goal; but I press on to make it my own, because Christ Jesus has made me his own. Beloved, I do not consider that I have made it my own; but this one thing I do:

forgetting what lies behind and straining forward to what lies ahead, I press on toward the goal for the prize of the heavenly call of God in Christ Jesus (Philippians 3:8–14).

V: Most high, all powerful, all good Lord! All praise is yours, all glory, all honor, and all blessing. To you, alone, Most High, do they belong. No mortal lips are worthy to pronounce your name.

R: All praise is yours, all glory, all honor, and all blessing.

V: Be praised, my Lord, through all your creatures, especially through my lord Brother Sun, who brings the day; and you give light through him. And he is beautiful and radiant in all his splendor! Of you, Most High, he bears the likeness.

R: All praise is yours, all glory, all honor, and all blessing.

V: Be praised, my Lord, through Sister Moon and the stars; in the heavens you have made them, precious and beautiful.

R: All praise is yours, all glory, all honor, and all blessing.

V: Be praised, my Lord, through Brothers Wind and Air, and clouds and storms, and all the weather, through which you give your creatures sustenance.

R: All praise is yours, all glory, all honor, and all blessing.

V: Be praised, My Lord, through Sister Water; she is very useful, and humble, and precious, and pure.

R: All praise is yours, all glory, all honor, and all blessing.

V: Be praised, my Lord, through Brother Fire, through whom you brighten the night. He is beautiful and cheerful, and powerful and strong.

R: All praise is yours, all glory, all honor, and all blessing.

V: Be praised, my Lord, through our sister Mother Earth, who feeds us and rules us, and produces various fruits with colored flowers and herbs.

R: All praise is yours, all glory, all honor, and all blessing.

V: Be praised, my Lord, through those who forgive for love of you; through those who endure sickness and trial. Happy those who endure in peace, for by you, Most High, they will be crowned.

R: All praise is yours, all glory, all honor, and all blessing.

V: Be praised, my Lord, through our Sister Bodily Death, from whose embrace no living person can escape. Woe to those who die in mortal sin! Happy those she finds doing your most holy will. The second death can do no harm to them.

R: All praise is yours, all glory, all honor, and all blessing.

V: Praise and bless my Lord, and serve him with great humility.

R: All praise is yours, all glory, all honor, and all blessing.

Let us pray:

Most High, glorious God, enlighten the shadows of our hearts, and grant to us a right faith, a certain hope, and perfect charity, so that we may accomplish your holy will. As we walk in the footsteps of St. Francis of Assisi, give us a spirit of poverty and humility so that we may be united with Jesus your Son in joy and in peace.

MISSION BASILICA

The Basilica is as grand as the Mission Chapel is humble. The spectacular nave ends with the apse and a high dome. Flanking the sanctuary to the left and right of the main altar area are two stands: The one on the left denotes the coat of arms for the diocese of San Francisco, and the cloth canopy on the right denotes this church as a minor basilica.

The basilica is filled with an amazing collection of stained glass windows. The large window at the rear with orange background depicts St. Francis, patron of the mission and the city of San Francisco. The upper side windows show angels with musical instruments. The lower side windows depict St. Junípero Serra,

Fr. Francisco Palóu, and the twenty-one missions of California, along with their patrons and founding dates.

The seven sorrows of Mary are carved on the front of the two side balconies, with the first sorrow carved over the main door at the rear of the church. The shrines throughout the church honor Sts. Anne and Mary, St. Martin de Porres, the Sacred Heart of Jesus, Our Mother of Perpetual Help, Our Lady of Guadalupe, Señor de los Milagros (Lord of Miracles, originally venerated in Lima).

Museum and Grounds

In the walkway approaching the museum stands a model of the mission as it would have looked around 1791. This diorama was first created for the 1939 World's Fair in San Francisco. The walkway also includes copies of drawings and photos from throughout the history of the mission. One famous photo shows the dancers from the various tribes gathering after Sunday Mass at the mission. The men have adorned themselves with feathers and paint their bodies with regular lines of black, red and white. They are dancing six or eight together, armed with spears, and expressing symbolic movements. Another later photo shows horse-drawn hearses carrying bodies for funeral services after the 1906 earthquake. Other photos hold memories of Pope John Paul II's visit to the mission in 1987.

Before entering the museum, notice the large tile mural by San Francisco artist Guillermo Granizo. It depicts the arrival of the ship *San Carlos* in San Francisco Bay. The upper left part of the mural shows the arrival of the Spanish military, Juan Bautista de Anza, and Fr. Junípero Serra, bringing the Christian Gospel to the natives. Fr. Serra holds in his hand a plan for Mission Dolores. The sails of the ship tell the story and consequences of their arrival: REY signifies the King of Spain's sponsorship of the colonization; DIOS expresses the faith brought by the Franciscan padres; PUEBLO indicates the city of San Francisco that would arise from this expedition; and MUERTE designates the gradual disappearance of the native peoples. The final sail asks a question: ¿QUIÉN SABE? (Who knows?) what would have happened if the expedition had not come to the land. The question is left for the reflection of the viewer. The green area surrounded by brown in the lower left-hand area of the mural represents the island of Alcatraz, and the pelicans, fish, and water express life in the San Francisco Bay.

In the museum, the inset in the wall shows how the mission was constructed. Father Cambon, who directed the building, reported that 36,000 adobe bricks were used to complete the project. In the central display are sacred artifacts: vestments, candlesticks, reliquaries, a monstrance, a hand bell, a tabernacle, and more. The displays of native life depict carvings, fire sticks for starting fires, a paddle for stirring food, baskets, ropes, duck decoys, mortar, bone tools, and decorations and jewelry carved from abalone shells.

Paintings in the museum depict St. Junipero Serra and Fr. Palóu, the two people most associated with the mission. One of the portraits shows Serra at the age of thirty-five embarking on his missionary career. It was executed by Lorenzo Ghiglieri in 1988 and used as the official image hung at St. Peter's Basilica at Serra's beatification.

Outside in the center of the cemetery stands a statue of St. Junípero Serra as sculpted by Arthur Putnam. Gradually the cemetery was consolidated to its present size, as unidentified bodies were reverently buried in a common grave amid redwoods, roses, cacti, and fragrant shrubs. Most of the marked graves come from the latter half of the nineteenth century after the mission era. Many of these early Californians have given their names to the streets of San Francisco.

OTHER NEARBY SIGHTS

Golden Gate Bridge. Because of its spectacular location, the Golden Gate Bridge is one of the world's most beautiful bridges. Opened in 1937, it spans the mile-wide strait between the Pacific Ocean and San Francisco Bay. The Golden Gate Strait was missed by the earliest European explorers—Cabrillo in 1542, Drake in 1579, and Vizcaino in 1602—probably because of its narrow passage and its ever-present fog. Only in 1769 did Gaspar de Portolá discover the strait and its bay, after which plans to colonize the area were set in motion.

The Presidio of San Francisco. The presidio was founded in 1776 near the Golden Gate. Then in 1794 the Spanish built El Castillo de San Joaquin, an adobe structure housing about a dozen cannons, on the promontory of white cliffs at the mouth of the gate to protect the bay against encroachment. The Americans would later build Fort Point on the same spot.

Today the area of the Presidio of San Francisco has been transformed into an urban park. The tail end of the overland trek led by Juan Bautista de Anza from Mexico to San Francisco is part of the extensive trail network of the park. From Mountain Lake in the southern end of the park, where the Anza expedition camped, the three-mile path leads northward to the Golden Gate Bridge. Fort Point, on the promontory next to the bridge, offers fabulous views of the entire bay area.

The entire Golden Gate National Recreation Area offers abundant opportunities for exploration, recreation, and some of the best sunsets to be witnessed anywhere.

"Mission of Bodily Healing"
Founded on December 14, 1817
1104 Fifth Avenue
San Rafael, CA 94901
www.saintraphael.com

This twentieth of the California missions was originally founded as a medical *asistencia* (sub-mission) of Mission San Francisco, to be used as a place for the sick to recover. On December 14, 1817, Fr. Vicente Francisco de Sarría rowed across the choppy bay with other Franciscans and more than two hundred ailing neophytes, to establish this convalescent hospital dedicated to God's healing messenger, Raphael the Archangel. The death rate of the neophytes at the San Francisco mission was increasing, and those who were ill were hindered in their recovery by the dense fog and damp winds of San Francisco. This "Mission of Bodily Healing" was sunnier and warmer, built with a southern exposure and buffered from the sea by wooded hills. San Rafael became the first sanitarium in California.

The Indian name for the site is Nanaguani, and it was inhabited by the Coast Miwok. On the day of its founding Mass, twenty-six native children were baptized and nearly two hundred adults enlisted for instructions in the faith. Fr. Gil y Taboada, being educated in medical science of the day, volunteered to minister at this new location. His success brought the number of neophytes there to 382 in the first year, as the sick were brought for healing. This was the scene on Easter of 1819, as recorded by Juan Garcia:

> Two days before Easter several thousand Indians began to arrive and set up camps all throughout the valley. Inside the

church the walls were banked on all sides with wild flowers. A procession of two hundred boys and girls were led by the missionaries through all the people to the church. As the procession passed, everyone knelt and chanted a prayer. At Mass the children received the sacrament of Confirmation. Later in the day many marriages were solemnized. For several days after Easter the Indians celebrated with feasting, horseback riding, and horse racing.[60]

Fr. Gil was replaced by Fr. Juan Amorós in 1819. He served the mission until his sudden death in 1832. As the site grew and prospered, it was granted full mission status on October 19, 1822. The friars taught the Indians to raise animals and grow fruits and vegetables. The natural springs on the hill above the mission provided irrigation for the orchards, vineyards, and fields of wheat, barley, beans, peas, and corn. Eventually the mission became self-sustaining, with a surplus of produce to trade. It became especially famous for its pears.

Mission San Rafael was the first mission to be secularized in 1834, and the chapel became the parish church for Mexican ranchers. The Mexican military commander Mariano Vallejo added the mission properties to his own holdings in the area and put many of the Indians to work for him. In 1846, General John C. Fremont captured the mission and used it as headquarters for the United States military forces. He used the chapel as a stable, and the old mission continued to deteriorate. In 1862, the buildings were demolished and replaced with a new parish church, the first of several frame churches on the site.

The present St. Raphael parish church was completed in 1919. In 1949, the Hearst Foundation provided funding to build a replica of the mission church. This current chapel is built on the approximate site of the original, although not oriented in the same direction as the original. Mission San Rafael Arcángel is today part of the active parish life of St. Raphael Church.

PATRON OF THE MISSION

San Rafael Arcángel (St. Raphael the Archangel) is one of the three archangels mentioned by name in Scripture and honored in the Church's liturgy. His name means "God heals," so he is an appropriate choice as patron of a mission originally intended as a place to recover one's health. He is a central character in the deuterocanonical book of Tobit, in which a just man, Tobit, is blind and unable to take the necessary journey to collect money he had deposited in faraway Media. He sends his son, Tobias, on the journey, and God sends the archangel Raphael in human disguise to accompany him. During the course of the journey the archangel's protective influence is shown in many ways.

When they reach the Tigris River, a fish leaps out to Tobias, and Raphael instructs Tobias to cut open and extract the heart, liver, and gall. In time they come to the house of Raguel, the father of Sarah, whom Tobias is destined to marry. However, a demon has killed every man Sarah married before the marriage could be consummated. Raphael instructs the young man to burn the fish's liver and heart to drive away the demon when he attacks on their wedding night. The two marry, and the fumes of the burning organs drive away the demon, whom Raphael follows and binds. Assuming that his new son-in-law will not survive the night, Sarah's father has begun digging his grave. But, surprised to find him alive and well in the morning, he orders a double-length wedding feast and has the grave filled. Since the feast prevents him from leaving, Tobias sends Raphael to recover his father's money.

After the feast, Tobias and Sarah return to the home of Tobit. There, Raphael tells Tobias to use the fish's gall to cure his father's blindness. Raphael then reveals his identity: "I am Raphael, one of the seven angels who stand ready and enter before the glory of the Lord" (Tobit 12:15). The archangel returns to heaven, and Tobit sings a hymn of praise.

The story was popular in the art of the mission period, especially the scenes of catching the fish and the healing of Tobit's blindness. When represented alone, Raphael is dressed as a winged traveler, sometimes holding a fish and a traveler's staff with a gourd tied to it. He is honored as a healing angel, a patron of travelers, and a protector of those with eye trouble. His feast is celebrated together with Sts. Michael and Gabriel on September 29.

MISSION BELLS

The bells hanging on a frame in front of the mission are replicas of the bells that were hanging there during the mission era. The frame in those days would have been made of timbers tied together rather than lumber bolted together. The original bells are now in the museum. The largest of the bells—and the oldest—dates from 1820, was made for San Rafael, and was hung by Fr. Amorós. The bell on top was obtained in 1833. The darker bell is an iron whaling bell that dates from 1831 and was also acquired for the mission in 1833. This bell is the first "tax-free" item imported into Marin County. Instead of going through the government or ecclesial authorities to get the bell, the padres negotiated directly with some whalers and so obtained the bell without any associated taxes.

MISSION CHURCH

The mission replica does not attempt to duplicate the original structure and is more of an estimation. The small plaque, to the right of the doorway, reads:

> Viva Jesus! "On the 14th of December 1817 Fra Ramon Abella, Narciso Durán, Luis Gil and I planted and blessed with solemn ceremonies the Holy Cross at the time of vespers, and on this day Holy Mass was sung with music *te deum* and the word of God was announced in both languages. In the afternoon there were 26 baptisms of children; we have about

200 for instructions." Report of Vicente de Sarria, Prefecto
to Mariano Payéras, Presidente.

The interior of the church is a simple, contemporary design. Above the altar is a statue of St.
Raphael the Archangel, with travel staff and
fish in his hand. To the left of the altar is a
statue of the Virgin Mary, and to the right, St.
Joseph. On the front of the ambo is a carving
of St. Raphael with a fish at his feet.

Above the simple Stations of the Cross are
mission-era paintings. On the right wall is a
nineteenth-century replica of the seventeenth-century original
by Giovanni Biliverti, *Tobias' Farewell to the Angel*. In this
scene at the end of the book of Tobit, the old man wishes to
thank the traveler for the return of his sight by offering him
rewards. His son, Tobias, also urges the traveler to take the treasure. The traveler refuses to accept and reveals his identity as
God's messenger, Raphael.

—PRAYER—

We adore You, Lord Jesus Christ, here, and in all your churches
throughout the whole world, and we bless You, because by your
holy Cross, You have redeemed the world (St. Francis of Assisi).

A READING FROM THE BOOK OF TOBIT:

"I was sent to you to test you. And at the same time God sent
me to heal you and Sarah your daughter-in-law. I am Raphael,
one of the seven angels who stand ready and enter before the
glory of the Lord." The two of them were shaken; they fell face
down, for they were afraid. But he said to them, "Do not be
afraid; peace be with you. Bless God forevermore. As for me,
when I was with you, I was not acting on my own will, but by
the will of God. Bless him each and every day; sing his praises.
Although you were watching me, I really did not eat or drink

anything—but what you saw was a vision. So now get up from the ground, and acknowledge God. See, I am ascending to him who sent me. Write down all these things that have happened to you." And he ascended. Then they stood up, and could see him no more. They kept blessing God and singing his praises, and they acknowledged God for these marvelous deeds of his, when an angel of God had appeared to them (Tobit 12:14–22).

V: St. Raphael, one of the seven angels who stand before the glory of God,

R: Pray for us.

V: St. Raphael, who offered to God the prayers of the father Tobit,

R: Pray for us.

V: St. Raphael, traveling companion of the young Tobias,

R: Pray for us.

V: St. Raphael, who delivered Sarah from evil and brought forth a happy marriage,

R: Pray for us.

V: St. Raphael, who healed the father Tobit of his blindness,

R: Pray for us.

V: St. Raphael, faithful guide and protector of those who travel,

R: Pray for us.

V: St. Raphael, health of the sick and joy of the sorrowful,

R: Pray for us.

V: St. Raphael, angel of those seeking a marriage partner and a happy marriage,

R: Pray for us.

V: St. Raphael, patron of those who care for the sick and minister God's healing,

R: Pray for us.

Let us pray:

O God, who created beings both visible and invisible, we praise you for the service and protection of your angels. Through the intercession of your archangel Raphael, guide us on our journey and guard us on our way. We pray for your merciful cure upon those most in need of the care of your angel Raphael, and we implore your healing from all our afflictions in body, mind, and spirit. May we rejoice with all your angels and saints as we praise your glory forever. Amen.

MUSEUM AND GROUNDS

Despite its small size, the museum contains a number of interesting artifacts from the mission era. It houses religious paintings and statuary, as well as several drawings and renditions of the original mission. The display includes altar vessels, religious books, musical scores, and three original mission bells.

Outside and to the right of the church is a life-size statue of St. Junípero Serra. Next to the statue is a boulder with a plaque dedicated to a Miwok native named Huicmuse. He was born in 1781 and baptized "Marino" at Mission San Francisco. Despite a life marked by armed rebellion against the Spanish colonists, he became Mission San Rafael's first *alcalde* (mayor). General Vallejo proposed this Miwok leader as the namesake for Marin County. The plaque reads:

> MARIN / Indian Warrior / Baptized by Franciscan fathers /
> a ferryman on the San Francisco bay / he became known as
> / EL MARINERO / (the sailor)

Both Chief Marin and Fr. Juan Amorós were buried on the mission grounds, although the location of their graves is now unknown. Further along the right side of the church is a large wooden cross that represents the cross erected to establish the mission.

Founded on July 4, 1823

114 E Spain Street

Sonoma, CA 95476

www.sonomaparks.org

The site for the mission was selected and conse-crated on July 4, 1823, by a young, ambitious Franciscan, Fr. José Altimira. The mission became the twenty-first establishment in the California chain, reaching finally from San Diego to Sonoma. It was both the last of the missions and the northernmost. The Sonoma mission seems to be more of an afterthought than part of the grand plan envisioned by St. Junípero Serra. Its short and raucous history is shared with the transition of California from the Spanish empire to part of newly independent Mexico.

Fr. Altimira, stationed at Mission San Francisco de Asís, was dissatisfied with the conditions: The climate was harsh, the soil sterile, and the converts few. He believed that a loca-tion with a warmer climate, north of the Bay area, would keep the neophytes healthier. With the support of Governor Luis Arguello and the Territorial Assembly in Monterey, but without official Church sanction, he intended to close down the mission establishments at San Francisco and San Rafael and move their people and goods to Sonoma. When word of the plan reached Father-President Sarria, Altimira was reprimanded and negotia-tions ensued. Fr. Sarria relented in part, agreeing to recognize the new mission, but vetoed the closure of the other missions. The Sonoma mission, rather than being called New San Francisco, would be dedicated to San Francisco Solano, a seventeenth-century missionary in Peru.

The site chosen for the mission was near the native village of Huchi in the area of the Coast Miwok people. The Pomo were to the northwest, the Wappo to the northeast, and the Suisunes and Patwin peoples to the east. The potential for gaining neophytes seemed abundant. With the help of seven hundred volunteer laborers from Mission Dolores, a wooden mission chapel was constructed and dedicated on April 4, 1824, when twenty-six Miwok children were baptized. In 1825, a long, low adobe wing with tiled roof was completed, containing living quarters, workshops, barracks, granary, and more. But Altimira proved to be a harsh overseer, and he was admonished by Church officials for too often punishing infractions through the use of the whip. Indian resentment grew, and in 1826 they set on fire the principal wooden buildings with much of the harvested grain. Fearing a native uprising, Altimira fled the mission and eventually returned to his native Spain.

A more experienced priest, Fr. Buenaventura Fortuni, was appointed to the mission and remained until 1833. He was both a fine administrator and a loving pastor, who gained the respect and trust of the Indian population. Under his direction, the mission reached its peak prosperity when nearly a thousand neophytes lived on the *rancherías*, more than seven thousand livestock grazed the land, and the agricultural output was abundant. He oversaw the construction of a large adobe church and the completion of a large mission quadrangle.

In 1834, the mission was secularized by the government, and its administration was turned over to General Mariano Vallejo, who commanded the Sonoma Barracks. Although the Spanish plan was to return the mission lands to the natives, the properties were absorbed into Vallejo's vast holdings. With the old mission as his headquarters, Vallejo established a pueblo named

Sonoma (Valley of the Moon). In 1840, the present chapel was constructed and furnished by Vallejo in order to provide Sonoma with a parish church, but after 1881 the chapel and its adjoining residence building were sold by the Church in order to build another parish church in a different part of the town. The buildings were then used variously as a hay barn, winery, and blacksmith shop. The property became a state monument when the Historic Landmarks League purchased them in 1903. Restoration work has been carried out in phases over the years, and the mission buildings today are maintained as a State Historical Park.

PATRON OF THE MISSION

San Francisco Solano (St. Francis Solano) was born in Montilia, Spain, in 1549. He became a member of the Franciscan order at age twenty and was ordained a priest seven years later. He was noted for his preaching, his care for and healing of the sick, and his talent as a violinist. As a young man, he described a saint as one who has emptied his or her heart of selfishness and has filled it with Christ.

In 1589, his request to serve as a missionary in South America was granted, and he sailed for Lima, Peru. For twenty years Solano worked at evangelizing the vast regions of Tucuman (present-day northwestern Argentina) and Paraguay. He was a remarkable linguist and learned many of the native tongues in order to preach the Gospel. Being a musician as well, Solano played the violin frequently for the natives, which endeared them to his message. On one occasion in the city of La Rioja, thousands of armed Indians approached the city to slay all Europeans and Christianized Indians. Courageously, Solano went out to meet them alone. He spoke eloquently, his words softening their hearts and disarming them of their weapons and ill intent. They then begged him for instructions, leading to the baptism of thousands.

He spent the last ten years of his life in Peru, where he became the guardian of the Franciscan friary in Lima. He died on July 14, 1610, and is considered to be the "Apostle of South America." He is usually depicted in a Franciscan habit and carrying a cross. Occasionally he is also shown with a violin or baptizing native peoples. St. Junípero Serra was in his teens when Solano was canonized in 1726, and, holding him in high esteem, had long desired that a mission be founded in Solano's name.

MISSION BELLS

A wooden bell frame outside the mission entrance holds one of the original bells. Dated 1829, six years after the founding of the mission, it is the only survivor of the original bells at the mission. It was cast in Mexico, and even though Mexico had taken over the territories from Spain, the bell still has the crown top. Apparently Mexican bell foundries kept using the old molds after independence from Spain.

MISSION CHURCH

The present church is an authentic restoration of the 1840 church, rebuilt in the early twentieth century. The simple façade is white, with deep brown wooden doors and lintels that top both the door and a window above.

The altar is simple, with a scene of the crucifixion of Christ in the center. Above is a framed portrait of San Francisco Solano, the patron of the mission, while the larger statues to the left and right are Mary in a red dress with black veil and Joseph in a green robe with gold cloak. The statues are simple, the type carved by local craftsmen. The sanctuary lamp and presider's chair date back to the days of the mission.

The chapel is painted in typical designs of the native people. The walls express the mountains and valleys of the land, and beneath runs a flowing image in blue that depicts the river of life. The brightly colored ceiling above the sanctuary and the vivid colors of the altar rail add to the intense effect. Paintings and Stations of the Cross line the side walls. At the back entry, below the niche for holy water, is a plaque that designates the tomb of "Maria Ygnacia Lopez Carrillo, buried here Feb 1849, Mother of Francisca Benicia Carrillo, who was the wife of General M.G. Vallejo."

—PRAYER—

We adore You, Lord Jesus Christ, here, and in all your churches throughout the whole world, and we bless You, because by your holy Cross, You have redeemed the world (St. Francis of Assisi).

A READING FROM THE LETTER OF ST. PAUL TO THE ROMANS: For one believes with the heart and so is justified, and one confesses with the mouth and so is saved. The scripture says, "No one who believes in him will be put to shame."

For there is no distinction between Jew and Greek; the same Lord is Lord of all and is generous to all who call on him. For, "Everyone who calls on the name of the Lord shall be saved."

But how are they to call on one in whom they have not believed? And how are they to believe in one of whom they have never heard? And how are they to hear without someone to proclaim him? And how are they to proclaim him unless they are sent? As it is written, "How beautiful are the feet of those who bring good news!" But not all have obeyed the good news; for Isaiah says, "Lord, who has believed our message?" So faith comes from what is heard, and what is heard comes through the word of Christ.

But I ask, have they not heard? Indeed they have; for
"Their voice has gone out to all the earth,
and their words to the ends of the world" (Romans 10:14–18).

V: St. Francis of Assisi proclaimed the Gospel in word and in deed.

R: "How beautiful are the feet of those who bring good news!"

V: St. Francis Solano evangelized the people of South America through native languages and beautiful music.

R: "How beautiful are the feet of those who bring good news!"

V: St. Junípero Serra was sent to bring the Gospel to the native peoples of California.

R: "How beautiful are the feet of those who bring good news!"

V: Missionary disciples today must announce the message of Christ and the Gospel of God's kingdom.

R: "How beautiful are the feet of those who bring good news!"

Let us pray:

O God, who gives your missionaries the zeal to bring the Good News of Jesus Christ to the nations, give us the desire to advance your kingdom wherever we may be. May we share a deep desire to show you more clearly to others, to love you more dearly in others, and to follow you more closely in all that we do each day of our lives. Amen.

MUSEUM AND GROUNDS

The first room of the museum is stocked with mission memorabilia, including a glass-enclosed section of the wall showing the original adobe bricks and a mission bell. The former dining room of the mission now showcases the paintings of Christopher Jorgensen, who depicted what remained of most of the

California missions when he painted them, from 1903 to 1905. The collection was donated by the artist's son, Virgil Jorgensen. The paintings generated a growing interest in preserving the missions in the early years of the twentieth century. The final room describes various facets of native and Spanish culture at the time of the missions.

The courtyard has been planted to show what might have been grown in the mission gardens. A flowing fountain, a covered cauldron for stirring beef fat while being rendered into tallow, a beehive oven for baking bread, and other items are featured. A large growth of Prickly Pear cactus stands in front of where the dormitory for unmarried girls stood, while beyond the court-yard there was a tannery for hides, vineyards, orchards, crops, and livestock.

To the left of the mission church, on the street side, lies a memorial to the 896 mission Indians who died and were buried during the short period of the mission's existence, from 1824 to 1839. Their Christian names are etched in polished black granite, as they were recorded by the priests in the mission records.

OTHER NEARBY SIGHTS

The Sonoma Barracks. Across the street from the mission, the barracks were built by General Vallejo in 1834, on orders from the new Mexican governor. He wanted to house a garrison in Sonoma to deter Russians from penetrating into California and to keep the local Indian tribes in check. Because secularization of the mission had been ordered that year, Vallejo was in charge of establishing the pueblo of Sonoma. Among the artifacts is a reproduction of the Bear Flag that was sewn and painted in the barracks to declare California's independence.

Sonoma Plaza. This plaza is the centerpiece of the town and a National Historic Landmark. The Bear Flag Revolt of June

14, 1846, was staged here, as Captain John Frémont raised the flag over the plaza and declared California free from Mexican rule. On July 9, the Bear Flag was replaced by the flag of the United States. Today, a monument to the revolt stands in the plaza. Other historical sites nearby include the Blue Wing Inn, the Toscano Hotel, La Casa Grande, and Lachryma Montis, the home of General Vallejo after 1850.

California Missions Museum. Ultimately, the mission vineyards have made the most lasting impression on visitors to this area. Winemaking, an important production for the mission, was an industry that has grown and flourished with private enterprises. The Sonoma Valley and the neighboring Napa Valley are renowned for their wines because the climate is perfect for growing a variety of grapes. The Cline Cellars winery contains the California Missions Museum, built to display a special set of mission models first shown at the Golden Gate International Exposition of 1939. These twenty-one intricately detailed models were built by German craftsmen under the direction of the Italian artist, Leon Bayard de Vale. The models were meticulously researched to represent each mission as it was originally built and designed by the missionaries. The museum also contains a figure of St. Junípero Serra, mission paintings by artists Robert Morris and Henry Nelson, and two stained-glass panels originally from Mission Dolores prior to the 1906 earthquake.

I express my gratitude to all the directors, archivists, custo-dians, and pastoral staff at each of the missions. They have been helpful in showing me hospitality and answering my inquiries. I am particularly grateful to Professor Robert Senkewicz at Santa Clara University for reading the manuscript and advising me on historical issues.

I am indebted to Heidi Saxton, editorial director at Servant, for guiding this work through the publishing process. Her many ideas and encouragement have created a much better book. I also thank Lynn Wehner for editing the book and making countless improvements to the text. Thanks also to the designer, Mark Sullivan, and marketing director, Louise Paré, and all who have had a role in bringing this book to publica-tion and promoting it.

I feel privileged to have encountered so many people involved with the California missions: preservationists, archivists, museum curators, foundation staff, as well as the bishops and pastoral staffs of the Catholic dioceses of California. Their work in maintaining the legacy of St. Junípero Serra and the missions of California continues to inspire and motivate me.

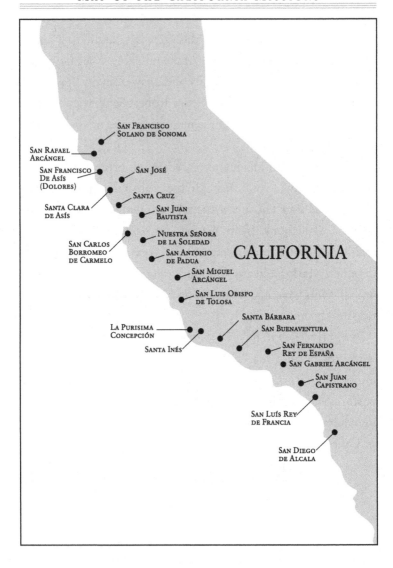

San Francisco
Solano de Sonoma

San Rafael
Arcángel

San Francisco
De Asís
(Dolores)

San José

Santa Cruz

Santa Clara
de Asís

San Juan
Bautista

Nuestra Señora
de la Soledad

San Carlos
Borromeo
de Carmelo

San Antonio
de Padua

CALIFORNIA

San Miguel
Arcángel

San Luis Obispo
de Tolosa

Santa Bárbara

La Purisima
Concepción

San Buenaventura

Santa Inés

San Fernando
Rey de España

San Gabriel Arcángel

San Juan
Capistrano

San Luís Rey
de Francia

San Diego
de Alcala

Founded by St. Junípero Serra

1. San Diego de Alcalá, July, 16, 1769
2. San Carlos Borromeo de Carmelo, June 3, 1770
3. San Antonio de Padua, July 14, 1771
4. San Gabriel Arcángel, September 8, 1771
5. San Luis Obispo de Tolosa, September 1,1772
6. San Francisco de Asís, June, 29, 1776
7. San Juan Capistrano, November 1, 1776
8. Santa Clara de Asís ,January 12, 1777
9. San Buenaventura, March 31, 1782

Founded by Padre Fermín Francisco Lasuén

10. Santa Barbara, December 4, 1786
11. La Purísima Concepción, December 8, 1787
12. Santa Cruz, August 28, September 25, 1791
13. Nuestra Señora de la Soledad, October 9, 1791
14. San José, June 11, 1797
15. San Juan Bautista, June 24, 1797
16. San Miguel Arcángel, July 25, 1797
17. San Fernando Rey de España, September 8, 1797
18. San Luis Rey de Francia, June 13, 1798

Founded by Others

19. Santa Inés, September 17, 1804
20. San Rafael Arcángel, December 14, 1817
21. San Francisco Solano, July 4, 1823

O God of the high heaven,

O Christ of the deep earth,

O Spirit of the flowing water,

O Trinity of love,

Who has called us to travel on pilgrimage,

on the Camino of St. Junípero Serra,

Bless the earth beneath our feet,

the way whereon we go, and the people whom we meet.

Guide us as you directed Abraham and Sarah to a new land,

as you led the people of Israel through the wilderness with cloud and fire,

as you urged Mary to the hill country, and pointed Paul to the nations.

Give us the heart of a pilgrim,

dependent on the hospitality of others and trusting in your presence.

Fill our hearts with joy,

freed from needless anxiety and lightened from the burdens of wealth.

Unbind us to live in your freedom,

focusing us on the things that matter most.

Bread of heaven, who feeds your people on their journey,

Living water, who quenches your people's thirsts,

nourish us along our pilgrimage way, with insights for our minds,

with fervor for our hearts, and with music for our souls.

Move in our lives, O God, during this pilgrimage,

As we leave our homes, the familiar and comfortable,

Liberate us to experience the Gospel through the encounter of
cultures.
Open our eyes to goodness and beauty,
Our ears to hear your voice speaking,
Our noses to the aromas of sanctity,
Our mouths to life's flavors and spices,
Our memories to savor all that you give us along the way.

God the Father who created us, give us a new birth,
God the Son who redeemed us, be our companion,
God the Holy Spirit who sanctifies us, lead the way before us,
May your blessings be with us on this journey, now and forever,
+ the Father, the Son, and the Holy Spirit. Amen.

1. "On the Road to San Diego: Junípero Serra's Baja California Diary," Rose Marie Beebe and Robert Senkewicz, trans. and ed. *The Journal of San Diego History*, vol. 59, no. 4 (Fall 2013), 206.
2. Maynard Geiger, *The Life and Times of Fray Junípero Serra: The Man Who Never Turned Back* (Washington, DC: Academy of American Franciscan History, 1959), vol. 1, 59.
3. Geiger, vol. 1, 191.
4. *Recopilación de Leyes de las Indias*, Ley 1, Titolo 1, Libro 5.
5. Serra to Antonia Maria Bucareli, May 21, 1773, in *Writings of Junipero Serra*, translated and edited by Antoine Tibesar (Washington, DC: Academy of American Franciscan History, 1955), vol. I, 363.
6. Serra to Fray Miguel de Petra, August 4, 1773, in *Writings of Junipero Serra*, vol. I, 391.
7. Serra to Antonia Maria Bucareli, December 15, 1775, in *Writings of Junipero Serra*, vol. II, 405.
8. Francisco Palou, *Francisco Palou's Life and Apostolic Labors of the Venerable Father Junipero*, translated by C. Scott Williams (Pasadena, CA: George Wharton James, 1913), 220.
9. Thomas of Celano, *First Life of St. Francis*, IV, 97.
10. Homily of His Holiness Pope Francis, Holy Mass and Canonization of Blessed Fr. Junipero Serra, National Shrine of the Immaculate Conception, Washington, DC, September 23, 2015.
11. Homily of His Holiness Pope Francis, Holy Mass and Canonization of Blessed Fr. Junipero Serra.
12. Homily of His Holiness Pope Francis, Holy Mass and Canonization of Blessed Fr. Junipero Serra.
13. Rose Marie Beebe and Robert M. Senkewicz, *Junípero Serra: California, Indians, and the Transformation of a Missionary* (Norman, OK: University of Oklahoma Press, 2015), 18–19.
14. Beebe and Senkewicz, 19.
15. Gregory Orfalea, *Journey to the Sun: Junipero Serra's Dream and the Founding of California* (New York: Scribner, 2014), 168.
16. Don De Nevi and Noel Francis Moholy, *Junípero Serra—The Illustrated Story of the Franciscan Founder of California's Missions* (New York: Harper and Row, 1985), 18.
17. Beebe and Senkewicz, 449.
18. Beebe and Senkewicz, 63.
19. Geiger, vol. 1, 220.
20. "On the Road to San Diego," 229.
21. Diary by Serra of the Expedition from Loreto to San Diego, June 26, 1769, in *Writings of Junipero Serra*, vol. I, 113.
22. To Father Juan Andres, written at San Diego, July 3, 1769, in *Writings of Junipero Serra*, vol. I, 139.
23. Serra to Father Juan Andres, written at Monterey, June 12, 1770, in *Writings of Junipero Serra*, vol. I, 169.
24. Geiger, vol. 1, 423–424.

25. Geiger, vol. 2, 71.
26. Beebe and Senkewicz, 320–321.
27. Serra to Antonia Maria Bucareli, Monterey, March 1, 1777, in *Writings of Junipero Serra*, vol. III, 113, 115.
28. Serra to Teodoro de Croix, Monterey, August 22, 1778, in *Writings of Junipero Serra*, vol. III, 253.
29. Beebe and Senkewicz, 369.
30. To Father Juan Sancho, written at Monterey, 1784, in *Writings of Junipero Serra*, vol. IV, 253.
31. Charles Edward Chapman, *A History of California: The Spanish Period* (New York: Macmillan, 1923), 358.
32. Geiger, vol. 2, 392.
33. Beebe and Senkewicz, 416.
34. Helen Hunt Jackson, "Father Junípero Serra and His Work," *Century Magazine* 26, no. 11, (May 1883), 3–18, 199–215.
35. George Wharton James, *Heroes of California: The Story of the Founders of the Golden State* (Boston: Little, Brown, and Company, 1910), 7–8.
36. John S. McGroarty, "San Diego: Where California Began," http://libraries.ucsd.edu/speccoll/DigitalArchives/f869_s22-s356-1915z/f869_s22-s356-1915z.pdf.
37. John F. Davis, *California Romantic and Resourceful; A Plea For The Collection, Preservation And Diffusion Of Information Relating To Pacific Coast History* (San Francisco: A.M. Robertson, 1914), 10–11.
38. Chapman, 353.
39. Isidore Dockweiler, *Acceptance and Unveiling of the Statues of Junipero Serra and Thomas Starr King*, Statuary Hall, US Capitol, Washington DC, 1931.
40. Maynard Geiger, *The Life and Times of Fray Junípero Serra: The Man Who Never Turned Back* (Academy of American Franciscan History, 1959), vol. 2, 402.
41. Cardinal Timothy Manning, gathered with the California bishops at Mission Carmel for the bicentennial year honoring the death of Serra, 1984.
42. President Ronald Reagan, letter to Thaddeus Shubsda, Bishop of Monterey, August 19, 1985.
43. Address of His Holiness John Paul II, Basilica of the Mission of San Carlos in Carmel, September 17, 1987.
44. Homily by Pope Francis at the Pontifical North American College, Rome, May 2, 2015.
45. Serra to Fray Francisco Palou, July 3, 1769, in *Writings of Junipero Serra*, vol. I, 141.
46. Francis J. Weber, "The Death of Fray Luis Jayme: Two Hundredth Anniversary," *Journal of San Diego History* 22, no. 1 (1976).
47. Letter to Fernando de Rivera y Moncada, October 5, 1776, translated and included in Beebe and Senkewicz, 333.
48. Diary entry for July 18, 1769, in Bolton, Herbert E., *Fray Juan Crespi: Missionary Explorer on the Pacific Coast, 1769-1774* (Berkeley, CA:

University of California, 1927), 129–130.

49. Zephyrin Engelhardt, OFM, *San Luis Rey Mission* (San Francisco: James H. Barry, 1921), 8.

50. Joseph Jeremias O'Keefe, OFM, *The Oceanside Blade*, X, no. 3 (January 1, 1898), 3, 12.

51. Vincent Fitzgerald, OFM, *St. John Capistran* (New York: Longmans, Green and Co., 1911), 114–115.

52. Sister Maria Philomena, MICM, "The Father of California: Saint Junípero Serra," December 6, 2008, http://catholicism.org/the-father-of-california.html.

53. "Prayers of Saint Bonaventure," Liturgies, http://www.liturgies.net/saints/bonaventure/prayer.htm.

54. *Francis of Assisi—The Saint: Early Documents,* vol. 1 (New York: New City, 1999), 163.

55. Palou, 110–114, 290.

55. Craig H. Russell, "Fray Juan Bautista Sancho: Tracing the Origins of California's First Composer and the Early Mission Style" Part II, *Boletín: Journal of the California Mission Studies Association*, vol. 21, Issue 2 (January 1, 2004), 9.

56. John Ross Browne, *Crusoe's Island: A Ramble in the Footsteps of Alexander Selkirk* (New York: Harper and Brothers, 1871), 177.

57. Clare of Assisi, "Third Letter to St. Agnes of Prague 12-14," *Francis and Clare: The Complete Works*, Regis J. Armstrong, OFM Cap., and Ignatius C. Brady, OFM, trans. (Mahwah, NJ: Paulist, 1982), 200.

58. Eugene Bolton Herbert, *Font's Complete Diary: A Chronicle of the Founding of San Francisco* (Oakland, CA: University of California, 1933), 341. Diary entry of Pedro Font written on March 28, 1776.

59. "Mission San Rafael History," Mission Tour.org, http://missiontour.org/wp/sanrafael/mission-san-rafael-history.html.

The California missions offer a new vocabulary that may be unfamiliar to many. Here is a list of terms and definitions that may be helpful when reading this book and while exploring the museums and grounds of the missions.

Adobe—Compound made of clay mixed with straw and sometimes dung. The mixture was pressed into molds and baked in the sun to form durable bricks. Also refers to structures made of this material.

Alabado—Hymn of praise, concluded the morning and evening prayer in the missions.

Alcalde—Neophyte appointed to assist the padres in keeping order, reinforcing the rules of the mission, and settling minor disputes.

Alta California—Upper California, now the state of California.

Ambo—Elevated pulpit, often reached with a flight of stairs, from which the Scriptures were read and sermons preached.

Arroyo—Creek or stream.

Asistencia—Sub-mission or branch mission. This was smaller than the main missions, usually consisting of a church, living quarters, workshops, and crops, but often without a resident priest.

Atole—Maize (cornmeal) gruel or porridge.

Baja California—Lower California, today the states of Baja California and Baja California Sur in Mexico.

Basilica—Church designated by the pope as having unique historical value or significance for pilgrimage. There are four major basilicas in Rome and minor basilicas designated throughout the world.

Bee-hive oven—Wood-fired cone-shaped oven used for baking bread. *Horno* in Spanish.

Bodega—Cellar for storing and maturing wine.

Bultos—Carved and painted sculptures of saints and other religious figures, usually set in a recess. Most of the mission churches featured a bulto depicting the saint for whom the mission is named.

Californio—Land owner of full or partial Hispanic heritage in California. Most Californios came from Mexico to settle in California.

Camino—Way, road, avenue, lane, path, trail, journey.

Campanario—Wall or tower, either free-standing or attached to a mission church, in which bells were hung.

Camposanto—Churchyard cemetery.

Cenotaph—Monument honoring a person or group of people whose remains are elsewhere.

Convento—Living quarters of the Franciscan friars, usually adjacent to the church.

Cuartel—Soldiers' quarters; barracks.

Doctrina—Compendium of Christian beliefs and prayers, usually recited by the neophytes each morning and evening.

El Camino Real—Literally "The Royal Way," designates the main road in a Spanish territory. As used in Alta California, it was the way that links the missions.

Façade—The face of a building, especially the principal front that looks onto a street or open space.

Fray—A title used with the full name of a friar. It could denote either a priest or a brother.

Friar—Member of a mendicant order, such as the Franciscans.

Gentile—Used by the Franciscans to designate those indigenous people who are not yet Christians.

Gente de Razón—Literally, "person of reason" (educated person), used to characterize non-Indians and those who followed Spanish customs.

Lavadero or lavanderia—A place for washing clothes and bathing.

Mayordomo—Foreman or supervisor of a mission under the priest.

Mestizo—Person of mixed European and Indian heritage.

Monstrance—Vessel for the exhibition of the consecrated host during Eucharistic adoration or Benediction of the Blessed Sacrament.

Monjerio—Dormitory for the unmarried neophyte girls at the mission.

Neophyte—A new believer; an Indian converted to Christianity and living at the mission.

Padre—"Father" in Spanish. A priest at the mission.

Pozole—Stew made of wheat, corn, beans, and meat.

Presidio—Fortified military outpost of Spanish soldiers who defended the lands around the missions.

Pueblo—Town or village established by Spanish-speaking settlers.

Quadrangle—Four-sided enclosure. The design used to lay out most of the missions.

Ranchería—Native village or settlement apart from the mission, usually consisting of non-permanent dwellings.

Rancho—Ranch, part of the mission territory for raising cattle and other animals, providing beef and leather for the mission communities and for trade.

Reredos—Altarpiece or decoration behind the altar in a church, usually featuring niches in which religious statuary is installed.

Sala—Formal reception room; an area in the mission used to receive guests and visitors.

Shaman—Person regarded as having access to, and influence in, the world of good and evil spirits, responsible among the Indians for curing disease and contacting the spiritual world.

Tabernacle or Sangrario—An ornamental vessel in a church for the reservation of the consecrated Eucharist.

Vaquero—Cowboy; a ranch hand who worked on the mission ranches.

Viceroy—Official appointed by the King of Spain, held responsible for civil, religious, and military affairs within vast overseas dominions. The missions in Alta California were under the authority of the Viceroy of New Spain, located in Mexico City.

Beebe, Rose Marie, and Robert M. Senkewicz. *Junípero Serra: California, Indians, and the Transformation of a Missionary.* Norman, OK: University of Oklahoma Press, 2015.

Engelhardt, Zephyrin. *The Missions and Missionaries of California* (multi-volume). San Francisco: James H. Barry, 1921.

Geiger, Maynard J. *Life and Times of Fray Junípero Serra OFM.* Washington, DC: Academy of American Franciscan History, 1959.

Hackel, Steven W. *Junípero Serra: California's Founding Father.* New York: Hill and Wang, 2013.

McLaughlin, David, and Ruben Mendoza. *The California Missions Source Book.* Scottsdale, AZ: Pentacle, 2012.

Orfalea, Gregory. *Journey to the Sun: Junípero Serra's Dream and the Founding of California.* New York: Scribner, 2014.

Palóu, Francisco. *Francisco Palóu's Life and Apostolic Labors of the Venerable Father Junípero Serra: Founder of the Franciscan Missions of California.* Pasadena, CA: George Wharton James, 1913.

Sandos, James A. *Converting California: Indians and Franciscans in the Missions.* New Haven, CT: Yale University Press, 2004.

Weber, Francis J. *Blessed Fray Junípero Serra: An Outstanding California Hero.* Eckbolsheim, France: Editions du Signe, 2008.

———. *The California Missions.* Eckbolsheim, France: Editions du Signe, 2005.